DRIVING STANDARDS AGENCY

DRIVING SKILLS

THE **Motorcycling Manual**

London: HMSO

Published by HMSO

© Crown copyright 1996
Applications for reproduction should be made to HMSO's
Copyright Unit

First edition Crown copyright 1991
Second edition Crown copyright 1996

ISBN 0 11 551781 2

British Library Catalogue in Publication Data
A CIP catalogue record for this book is available from the
British Library

Other titles in the *Driving Skills* series

The Complete Theory Test for Cars and Motorcycles
The Theory Test for Large Vehicle Drivers (forthcoming)
The Driving Test
The Driving Manual
The Bus and Coach Driving Manual
The Goods Vehicle Driving Manual
The Theory Test and Beyond (CD-ROM)

The Driving Standards Agency (DSA) would like to thank the following for their assistance

- Department of Transport, Road Safety Division
- The staff of the Driving Standards Agency

CONTENTS

Motorcycling can be a pleasant and exhilarating experience, as well as an economic means of transport. However, the volume of traffic and faster, more powerful motorcycles make it essential, more than ever before, for riders to be ready to deal with the unexpected and question the actions of other road users. After all, it's in your interest to make safety *your* responsibility.

The Driving Standards Agency (DSA) is an agency of the Department of Transport. Its primary aim is to promote road safety in Great Britain through the advancement of driving standards. This manual is designed to help motorcyclists at all levels of experience to master safe riding as a life skill.

Whether you're an experienced motorcyclist or a new rider you'll realise that riding not only requires skill in handling your machine but also the ability to 'read' the road. Good observation and anticipation are essential to safe riding.

This book is a step-by-step guide to motorcycling, covering all aspects: from choosing your machine and the correct protective clothing to defensive riding and the importance of proper training. It's an essential reference book for all motorcyclists, however experienced – instructors too. Read it carefully and put into practice the advice it gives.

Above all, make sure that your aim is *Safe driving for life*.

Robin Cummins
The Chief Driving Examiner
Driving Standards Agency

Riding a motorcycle can be great fun and is enjoyed by people of all ages. However, riding on the road means accepting responsibility for yourself.

Compared with driving other road vehicles, riding a motorcycle puts you at greater risk from other road users. If you're involved in an accident the chances of injuring yourself are **very** high.

The machine, the special clothing, the road, the weather, and the traffic are all part of the environment of motorcycling. How well you get on depends on *you*.

This part covers the attitude and approach you need to ensure that you enjoy a long and safe motorcycling career.

The topics covered

* **Your attitude**
* **Economy**

Your attitude

The attitude you take to motorcycling will influence the type of rider you become. Always try to set a good example by showing

- Responsibility
- Anticipation
- Patience
- Concentration
- Expertise

Take pride in your riding and you'll develop a positive attitude. This won't always be easy but keep working at it.

It's a fact that nearly all road accidents are caused by human error. Reducing that risk is the responsibility of us all.

DSA THE MOTORCYCLING MANUAL

Responsibility

To be a responsible rider you should always be concerned for the safety of all road users.

This includes

- Yourself and your passenger
- Other drivers and riders
- Cyclists
- Pedestrians, particularly the most vulnerable such as
  - children
  - the elderly
  - people with disabilities

Be responsible by recognising your own limitations. Riding beyond the bounds of caution is foolish and irresponsible.

Develop the right attitude from the beginning and you'll become a safe and responsible rider.

Anticipation

When you're riding a motorcycle it's vital that you plan ahead. This means acting before situations get out of control. As a motorcyclist you have to consider

- Other road users. They don't always do what you expect. Question their actions and be ready for the unexpected.
- The road. How sharp is the next bend? What's around the next corner? Can you stop within your range of vision? Road signs and road markings are there to help you plan ahead
- The conditions. You'll be exposed to the weather and affected by the road conditions. Slippery surfaces are especially dangerous for motorcyclists

Anticipation is a skill which develops with experience. In time it should become second nature.

Patience

Try not to over-react if another road user does something wrong. Control your desire to retaliate. Everyone can make a mistake and it's not your place to teach a bad driver a lesson.

Showing good manners is the hallmark of a skilful rider. Others will learn from watching you and will appreciate your courtesy and good riding.

Traffic jams and delays can cause frustration. Avoid the need to rush. Set out with plenty of time to spare. It's always better to arrive late than not at all.

Concentration

Riding on today's roads demands full concentration.

If you're driving a car a lapse in concentration may only dent your pride (and your car). Motorcycles aren't so forgiving. Your survival will depend on your concentration.

Many factors can disrupt your concentration such as

- Feeling tired or unwell
- Being cold or wet
- Worries
- Alcohol
- Drugs

It's in your own interest not to ride if you know you can't concentrate fully.

Feeling tired or unwell   Health is one personal matter which can upset your concentration. A bad cold can distract your mind and slow your reactions. If you feel tired or unwell don't ride.

Cold and wet   Without proper clothing you can get very cold and wet when riding a motorcycle. Hands and feet are especially susceptible. Being cold and wet will reduce your ability to concentrate and slow your reactions.

Worries   If something upsets or worries you think twice before starting a journey. If you can't concentrate on your riding consider using some other means of transport.

Alcohol   This will reduce your ability to ride safely. The law sets the limit of 80 milligrams of alcohol per 100 millilitres of blood. It's an offence to ride a motorcycle or a moped if you exceed this level.

If you want to be safe and you're going to ride don't drink at all.

Drugs Taking certain drugs is a criminal offence. Riding when you're under their influence can seriously impair your concentration. The outcome could be fatal.

If your doctor prescribes medicines for you ask if they'll affect your ability to ride safely. Some over-the-counter medicines can also affect you. Read the label. If in doubt ask the chemist or your doctor.

The responsibility is yours.

Warning Riding under the influence of alcohol or drugs could invalidate your insurance.

Expertise

Master the techniques set out in this manual. They were developed by experienced riders and they make sense.

Develop safe habits and a responsible attitude from the very beginning. Always think about how other road users will be affected by your actions.

Think 'Safety'.

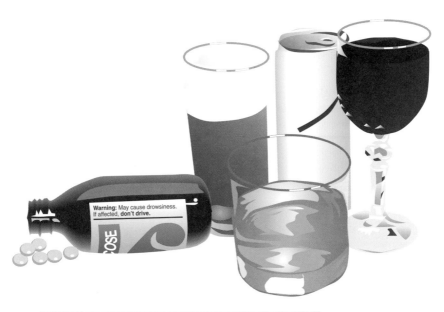

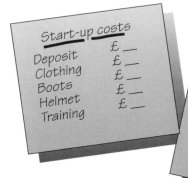

Start-up costs

Deposit   £ __
Clothing   £ __
Boots   £ __
Helmet   £ __
Training   £ __

Budget

Monthly loan repayments (x 12)   £ __
'Road Tax'   £ __
Insurance   £ __
Petrol   £ __
Oil   £ __
Maintenance   £ __
Tyres   £ __
Misc.   £ __
Total for year   £ __
Monthly cost   £ __

Economy

Motorcycling is traditionally a cheap form of transport. However, if you're a beginner you must accept that there are considerable start-up costs.

Don't cut costs to below the minimum level of safety. For example, don't risk using worn or damaged tyres. Safety must never be sacrificed for economy.

Running some motorcycles can be more expensive than running some types of car.

Set yourself a budget so that you know what you can afford. This will help you to identify where savings can be made.

You'll have to consider

- The purchase price of the motorcycle

- The vehicle excise duty and insurance

- The cost of proper clothing

- The cost of training

- The running costs: fuel, maintenance, etc.

You have to comply with certain legal requirements before you can ride on the road. These requirements fall into two categories

- Those with which you must comply

- Those with which you must ensure your motorcycle complies

Most of the requirements are there to protect you and other road users. If you neglect them you could face serious penalties. Complying with the law isn't cheap but failing to comply could turn out to be much more expensive.

The topics covered

- **The driving licence**
- **Compulsory Basic Training (CBT)**
- **Types of licence**
- **Motorcycle and moped licence requirements**
- **Foreign licence-holders**
- **Vehicle documents**
- **Insurance**

The driving licence

The law governing driving licences for motorcyclists can appear complicated. This section explains how the law affects you.

Legal requirements

To ride a motorcycle on the road you must

*   Be at least 17 years old
*   Have a driving licence which allows you to ride motorcycles (category A)

That licence can be any of the following

*   A provisional driving licence with motorcycle entitlement
*   Full car licence. This automatically provides provisional motorcycle entitlement
*   Full motorcycle licence
*   Full moped licence. This provides automatic provisional motorcycle entitlement if you're aged 17 years or over

Provisional motorcycle entitlement

This entitles learners to ride a solo motorcycle

*   Up to 125cc
*   With a maximum power output of 9kW

From 1 January 1997 learners may ride solo motorcycles

*   Up to 125cc
*   With a maximum power output of 11kW

Learners who wish to ride a side-car outfit can do so with a power to weight ratio not exceeding 0.16kW/kg.

If you aren't sure ask for advice from your motorcycle dealer.

With provisional motorcycle entitlement you must not

*   Ride on motorways
*   Carry a pillion passenger
*   Ride without L plates. In Wales you may display a red D plate (for *Dysgwr*, the Welsh for 'learner'). If you cross from Wales into England you must display L plates.

Two-year limit

Motorcycle entitlement on a provisional licence lasts for two years. You must pass the motorcycle test within that time or your entitlement will expire. You'll then have to wait one year before you can have motorcycle entitlement again.

Compulsory Basic Training (CBT)

You must satisfactorily complete a CBT course before you're allowed to ride on the road, unless you hold a licence with provisional motorcycle entitlement which started before 1 December 1990.

From 1 January 1997 all learner motorcyclists and moped riders must complete CBT before riding on the road. This includes riders who hold either a pre-1 December 1990

- Full car licence with provisional motorcycle entitlement
- Provisional moped licence

You don't have to take CBT if you

- Have passed a full moped test
- Live and ride on specified offshore islands
- Already hold a Certificate of Completion (DL196) obtained during a previous motorcycle entitlement or when riding a moped

When you've completed CBT you'll be given a DL196. Keep this safe. You must have a DL196 before you can take the practical motorcycle test.

From 1 July 1996 CBT certificates have a three-year life. This means

- Certificates issued before that date will have a three-year life from 1 July 1996
- Certificates issued on or after that date will have a three-year life from their date of issue

A DL196 obtained on a moped is valid for a motorcycle when the rider reaches the age of 17.

Types of licence

From 1 January 1997 there are two types of full motorcycle licence to aim for.

Light motorcycle licence (category A1)

If you pass your test on a motorcycle of between 75 and 125cc you'll obtain a full light motorcycle licence. This will provide full licence entitlement on any motorcycle up to 125cc and with a power output of up to 11kW (14.6 bhp). If your test machine is between 120 and 125cc **and** capable of 100 kph you'll attain the full category A standard motorcycle licence.

Standard motorcycle licence (category A)

Your test motorcycle must be over 120cc but no larger than 125cc. It must be capable of at least 100 kph. Your full standard motorcycle licence will be subject to the two-year qualifying period (see Note 4).

If you pass your test on a motorcycle with automatic or semi-automatic transmission this will be recorded on your licence. Your full licence entitlement will be restricted to motorcycles in this category.

If you're using either the accelerated access or direct access schemes your test motorcycle must be of at least 35kW (46.6 bhp).

Full licence entitlements

With a full motorcycle licence you may

- Ride without L plates (or D plates in Wales)
- Carry a pillion passenger
- Use motorways

Theory test transitional arrangements

After 1 January 1997 it will be necessary to pass the theory test before a booking for a practical test will be accepted. However, between 1 July and 31 December 1996 there will be a special arrangement to allow candidates to take the practical test first, if necessary. To gain a full licence the theory test must then be passed within six months.

Motorcycle and moped licence requirements

The table on the following pages provides a quick method of seeing how the law affects you from 1 January 1997. The following notes contain additional information and are referred to in the table.

Note 1:
Theory test

A theory test pass certificate is valid for two years.

Note 2:
Accelerated access

This option is for riders over 21 years old or who reach the age of 21 before their two-year qualifying period is complete (see Note 4).

You can take a further test to give you immediate access to all motorcycles. This test must be taken on a motorcycle with a power output of at least 35kW (46.6 bhp).

You can practise for this test on motorcycles above 25kW (33 bhp) provided

- You're accompanied at all times by an approved instructor, on another motorcycle and in radio contact
- Fluorescent or reflective safety clothing is worn during supervision

- L plates (or D plates in Wales) are fitted and provisional licence restrictions followed

Note 3:
Direct access

This option is open to learner riders aged 21 or over.

You can take one test to give you direct access to any size of motorcycle. The test must be taken on a motorcycle of at least 35kW (46.6 bhp).

You can practise on any size of motorcycle. If you practise on a motorcycle which exceeds the UK learner specification

- You must be accompanied at all times by an approved instructor, on another motorcycle and in radio contact
- Fluorescent or reflective safety clothing must be worn during supervision
- L plates (or D plates in Wales) must be fitted and provisional licence restrictions followed

Note 4:
Two-year qualifying period

After obtaining the full standard category A licence you may

- Ride on motorways
- Carry a pillion passenger
- Ride without L plates (or D plates in Wales)

However, you're restricted to motorcycles up to 25kW (33 bhp) and a power to weight ratio not exceeding 0.16kw/kg for two years. After two years you may ride any size of motorcycle without taking another test.

Note 5:
Moped riders

To ride a moped on the public road you must

- Be at least 16 years old
- Have a driving licence that entitles you to ride mopeds (category P)

That licence can be any of the following

Aged 16 but under 17

- Full moped licence
- Provisional moped licence

Aged 17 and over

As above but also

- Full car or motorcycle licence. (These provide full moped entitlement.)
- A provisional driving licence. (This provides automatic provisional moped entitlement.)

Note   Provisional moped entitlement is not subject to the two-year limit.

Provisional moped entitlement
allows you to ride a machine which

- Has an engine under 50cc
- Has a maximum design speed not exceeding 30 mph
- Doesn't weigh more than 250kg
- Can be moved by pedals if the moped was registered before 1 August 1977

Full moped licence entitlement
allows you to

- Ride mopeds without L plates (or D plates in Wales)
- Carry a pillion passenger

Note 6:
Minimum test vehicles (MTVs)

- Motorcycles less than 75cc aren't acceptable for the practical motorcycle test

- Only the disabled can use a motorcycle and side-car combination for the test. The licence obtained will be restricted to such combinations

- If you pass your test on a motorcycle with automatic or semi-automatic transmission this will be recorded on your licence. Your full licence entitlement will be restricted to motorcycles in this category

- A full light motorcycle licence will give you full licence entitlement to ride machines up to 125cc and with a power output of up to 11kW

Light motorcycle MTV

Standard motorcycle MTV

Accelerated/direct access MTV

How to attain a full motorcycle licence from 1 January 1997

Type of licence currently held	CBT required
Provisional licence with motorcycle entitlement	**Yes,** before you can ride on the road
Full car licence	**Yes,** before you can ride on the road
Full motorcycle licence, and subject to the two-year qualifying period *(see Note 4)*	**No**
Full moped licence	**No**

How to attain a full moped licence from 1 January 1997 *(Note 5)*

Provisional moped licence (aged 16)	**Yes,** before you can ride on the road
Provisional licence	**Yes,** before you can ride on the road

Minimum test vehicles *(see Note 6)*	Engine
Moped	Under 50cc
Light motorcycle (A1)	75–125cc
Standard motorcycle	120–125cc
Accelerated access	Unspecified
Direct access	Unspecified

Theory test required *(see Note 1)*	Accelerated access *(see Note 2)*	Direct access *(see Note 3)*
Yes, before you take the practical test	Not applicable	Available if you're aged 21 or over
No	Not applicable	Available if you're aged 21 or over
No	Available if you're aged 21 or over	Not applicable
Yes, unless you obtained your full moped licence by taking a two-part theory/practical test	Not applicable	Available if you're aged 21 or over
Yes, before you take the practical **moped** test	Not applicable	Not applicable
Yes, before you take the practical **moped** test	Not applicable	Not applicable

Power	Speed
	30 mph max. (and doesn't weigh more than 250 kg)
11kW (14.6 bhp) max.	Not capable of exceeding 100 kph (62.5 mph)
11kW (14.6 bhp) max.	Capable of exceeding 100 kph (62.5 mph)
35kW (46.6 bhp) min.	Unspecified
35kW (46.6 bhp) min.	Unspecified

Foreign licence-holders

Visitors or new residents

Visitors to Great Britain or new residents can drive on their foreign licence or International Driving Permit (IDP) for up to 12 months.

You must make sure that

- Your licence or IDP is valid
- You have entitlement for the size of motorcycle you intend to ride
- You're aged 17 or over

You must apply for a UK licence before riding if

- You don't have the correct motorcycle entitlement
- You've been in Great Britain for more than 12 months

If you want to take a motorcycle test you'll have to hold a UK provisional licence or counterpart before you take

- The theory test
- The practical motorcycle test

European Community and other driving licences

EC licences are valid for driving in the UK until they expire. Licences from designated countries can be exchanged for a UK licence within 12 months without the need to take a test.

If your motorcycle entitlement was granted automatically when you passed a test in a car or other vehicle, however,

- You'll be given full moped entitlement and provisional motorcycle entitlement
- You'll have to pass a motorcycle test to have full motorcycle entitlement

Information Leaflet D100 'What You Need to Know about Driver Licensing' gives further information about foreign licences available for exchange. This is available at larger post offices or you can get further advice from The Driver Enquiry Unit, The Driver and Vehicle Licensing Agency (DVLA), Swansea SA6 7JL. Tel: 01792 772151.

Vehicle documents

The registration document (VRD)

This contains details of your motorcycle

- Make and model
- Year of first registration
- Engine size and number

It also gives your name and address.

If you buy a new machine the dealer will register your motorcycle with the DVLA. A registration document will then be sent directly to you from the DVLA.

If you buy a second-hand machine you'll receive the VRD from the previous owner. Fill in the 'Change of ownership' section and send it off to the DVLA at the address given on the document. You should do this immediately as it's an offence not to notify the DVLA.

Vehicle excise duty

This is often called 'road tax' or the 'vehicle licence'. You must display the vehicle excise licence ('tax disc') on the vehicle.

Applying You can get the vehicle licence application form at any post office. Follow the instructions on the form. Most main post offices can accept your application.

The fee This varies with engine size. These classes are

- Up to 150cc
- 151–250cc
- Over 250cc

Documents When you apply to renew your vehicle excise licence you must produce

- A vehicle test certificate (MOT) if your motorcycle is three years old and over
- A valid certificate of insurance
- An excise licence renewal form

Older motorcycles Motorcycles over 25 years old don't have to pay vehicle excise duty but should display a 'nil' disc.

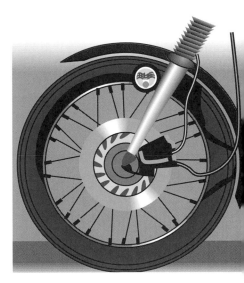

The vehicle test certificate (MOT)

The MOT test applies to all motorcycles, mopeds and scooters over three years old. The test must be carried out every year at an appointed vehicle testing station. For motorcycles this is often, but not always, a motorcycle dealer.

Purpose of the test

The test is to check that your motorcycle is roadworthy at the time it's tested.

It's always the rider's responsibility to ensure that

* Any fault which develops is promptly corrected

* Any machine you're riding is roadworthy

When your machine passes the test you'll be given a vehicle test certificate. You'll need to produce this document when you renew your vehicle excise licence.

If your motorcycle fails you must not ride it on the road unless you're taking it

* To have the failure faults corrected

* By prior appointment for a retest at the vehicle testing station

When to test You can have your motorcycle tested

* Up to one month before it's three years old

* Up to one month before the current certificate runs out. If you do this your new certificate will expire one year after the expiry date of the old one

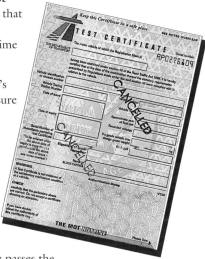

Insurance

It's illegal to ride without insurance. Should you cause injury to anyone or damage property it could result in prosecution.

Before you take a motorcycle onto public roads get proper insurance cover. You can arrange this through

- The insurance company directly
- A broker
- A motorcycle dealer
- The manufacturer (sometimes)

The insurance company Insuring directly with an insurance company is probably a little cheaper than the same policy through a broker. Finding the best deal, however, can be a time-consuming business.

A broker Many brokers are linked by computer to the main insurance companies. This allows them to get comparative quotes very quickly. A good broker will shop around and find the best policy for you.

If you already have car insurance ask your present insurer first.

A motorcycle dealer A dealer can act as a broker or may have a direct link with an insurance company. Sometimes the dealer can offer insurance deals through the manufacturers.

The manufacturer Some larger manufacturers make arrangements with insurance companies. This benefits the motorcyclist by offering competitive rates. Your dealer will be able to tell you about cover in this category.

Types of Insurance

Third party This type of insurance is the legal minimum and the cheapest cover.

The 'third party' is any person you might injure or property you might damage. You aren't covered for damage to your motorcycle or injury to yourself.

If you damage a car the owner could claim against you. On the other hand, if someone damaged your motorcycle you could claim against them.

Third party fire and theft This is the same as third party but it also covers you for

- Your motorcycle being stolen
- Damage by fire

Comprehensive This is the best, but the most expensive insurance. Apart from covering other persons and property from injury and damage this covers

- Damage to your machine
- Replacement of parts damaged in an accident
- Personal injury to yourself

Pillion passenger insurance All policies include cover for a pillion passenger. This is much the same as for motor car passengers.

The cost of insurance

This varies with

- Your age – the younger you are, the more it will cost
- The make of your motorcycle
- The power and capacity of the engine
- Where you live

Engine-size groups for insurance purposes can vary from one insurer to another. This is another reason to shop around when looking for insurance cover.

What's insured

This also varies from company to company. Read the small print and ask your insurer or broker.

You'll often have to pay the first £50 or £100 of any claim. This is called the 'excess'.

Shop around and buy the best policy you can afford.

The certificate of insurance

This is a short and simple document which certifies

- Who is insured
- The type of vehicle covered
- The kind of insurance cover
- The period of cover
- The main conditions

Sometimes a broker will give you a temporary certificate or 'cover note'. This is issued while you're waiting for your certificate and is proof of insurance.

Keep the certificate safe and produce it

- If the police ask you
- When you apply to renew your vehicle excise licence

The policy document

This contains the full details of the contract between you and the insurance company. It's usually written in legal language. Ask your broker or the insurance company to explain any details which you don't understand.

POLICE ACCIDENT

Accidents

If you're involved in an accident the law requires you to

- Stop at the scene
- Give your name and address to anyone having cause to ask for it
- Give the motorcycle owner's name and address (if different)
- Give the registration number of the machine
- Give the name and address of your insurer

You must notify the police if

- Any person is injured (however slightly)
- You've been unable to give your details at the scene of the accident

In cases where you must notify the police this must be

- As soon as possible, or
- Within 24 hours of the accident

Motorcycles come in many different types and sizes. You need to think carefully before deciding which one to buy. Buying one that doesn't suit your needs can be a costly mistake and could spoil your enjoyment of motorcycling.

Apart from buying the machine you'll have to consider

- Insurance
- Running costs
- Clothing

This part looks at what you need to consider when buying a motorcycle. It also describes the various types of motorcycle and their main features.

The topics covered

- **Buying a motorcycle**
- **Mopeds**
- **Learner motorcycles**
- **Automatic motorcycles**
- **Commuter motorcycles**
- **Sports motorcycles**
- **Touring motorcycles**
- **Custom motorcycles**
- **Off-road motorcycles (trail bikes)**

Buying a motorcycle

When you're thinking about buying a motorcycle you need to consider

- Your budget
- The type of motorcycle you would like
- The location of the nearest dealer

You'll also want to know where to get advice if you need it.

Budget

Costs you'll have to think about include

- **Purchase price** This may determine whether you buy new or second-hand
- **Insurance** Some models cost a lot more to insure than others
- **Running costs** Fuel consumption, tyres and the cost of spare parts need to be considered
- **Clothing** If you're new to motorcycling the cost of a helmet, gloves, jacket, boots, etc. can be a major consideration

Type of motorcycle

When choosing a machine you'll need to ask yourself about

- **Your licence** Are you entitled to ride motorcycles of any engine size?

- **Suitability** What do you want from your motorcycle? A commuter machine is going to struggle with long-distance motorway riding
- **Comfort** Are you comfortable on the machine? Can you reach the controls easily? Can your feet reach the ground?
- **Weight** Some motorcycles are very heavy. This can present problems when parking or manoeuvring

Motorcycle dealers

The motorcycle dealership in your area could influence your decision. Being able to have your machine serviced locally could be important to you. A dealer can also

- Offer finance packages
- Offer part exchange deals
- Offer special insurance rates
- Arrange training courses
- Let you try out a motorcycle before you make a final decision (subject to your licence entitlement)
- Give you expert advice

Further information

You can get further information from manufacturers' brochures, magazines and newspapers. Talking to other riders can give you another viewpoint. However, at the end of the day, the final choice is always yours.

Mopeds

A moped is a motorcycle which

- Must not have an engine over 50cc

- Can't go faster than 30 mph

- Doesn't weigh more than 250kg

- Can be moved by pedals, if the moped was registered before 1 August 1977

A moped can be ridden without L plates (or D plates in Wales) by people who hold a full car, moped or motorcycle licence.

Learner motorcycles

These motorcycles are suitable for use by learners provided

- The engine isn't over 125cc

- The engine power output doesn't exceed 9kW (11kW (14.6 bhp) after 1 January 1997)

- L plates (or D plates in Wales) are fitted both to the front and back of the machine

(These engine-size restrictions don't apply to learners under the accelerated or direct access schemes. See Part Two.)

Automatic motorcycles

Automatic or semi-automatic motorcycles have automatic transmission. They're usually small and easy to ride. You can take your motorcycle test on one of these machines. If you pass your full licence entitlement will be restricted to such machines.

Automatic motorcycles are ideal for short trips and for use in heavy town traffic.

Commuter motorcycles

Any motorcycle could be used for taking you to and from work. Commuter machines are especially suitable for commuting shorter distances. They're

- Economical to run
- Lightweight and easy to ride
- Low-powered
- Available with automatic, semi-automatic and manual transmissions

Sports motorcycles

These motorcycles have road racing styling. They come in a variety of engine sizes and are

- Expensive to buy and run
- Capable of very high speed
- Suitable for long-distance riding at motorway speeds

When you ride this type of machine for the first time take care. You may find yourself going faster than you intended.

Touring motorcycle

Touring motorcycles are designed for comfortable long-distance riding. They feature

- A relaxed riding position
- Luggage carrying capacity
- Often some form of fairing for weather protection
- A large engine size

Despite their size and weight these motorcycles are capable of continuous high speeds.

Custom motorcycles

Custom motorcycles are recognisable by their unique styling. Custom motorcycles

- Are available in a wide range of engine sizes, including 125cc

- Usually have a low seat height

- Have a 'laid-back' riding position

Off-road motorcycles (trail bikes)

Trail bikes are designed so that they can be used both on and off the road. This type of motorcycle

- Comes in a wide range of engine sizes

- Has extra ground clearance, which increases the seat height

- Is fitted with dual-purpose tyres

- Is built to cope with riding over rough ground

Without the right clothing you can get very cold and wet when riding a motorcycle. Special motorcycling clothing is available which

- Protects you from the weather
- Helps to protect you from some types of injury
- Helps other road users to see you

The topics covered

- **Protective clothing**
- **Gloves and gauntlets**
- **Boots**
- **Visibility aids**
- **Safety helmets**
- **Visors and goggles**
- **Motorcycle fairings**
- **Windscreens**
- **Handlebar muffs**

Protective clothing

Clothing is available which will keep you warm and dry in all but the worst conditions. If you allow yourself to become cold and wet when riding you'll lose concentration.

Protective clothing for motorcyclists is designed to protect you from

- The cold and wet
- Some kinds of injury

Clothing for which a manufacturer either claims or implies protection, other than from the weather, must be marked with the 'C E' mark.

Motorcycle protective clothing is of two main types

- Clothing made from man-made materials
- Leather clothing

Man-made materials

To protect you from the weather nylon is the most popular material. It's available in many different forms and comes under many different brand names. Other materials such as waxed cotton and PVC are also available.

More expensive garments have reinforcing and padding at the shoulders and elbows. This provides some protection in the event of an accident.

Generally, man-made outer clothing is designed to fit over your normal clothes and comes as either

- A jacket and trousers
- A one-piece suit

These can be either lined or unlined.

When you're buying outer clothing make sure that

- You have enough room for extra layers of warm clothing underneath
- Your movement isn't restricted

Leathers

Motorcyclists have traditionally worn leathers. They offer a high degree of protection from gravel burns if you fall off. Motorcycle leathers come as

- One-piece suits
- Two-piece zip-together suits
- Separate jacket and trousers

These can be lined or unlined.

One-piece suits Leather motorcycle suits aren't designed to fit over your normal clothes. They do, however, offer the motorcyclist certain advantages

- Reduced wind resistance
- A high degree of windproofing

They also have some disadvantages

- Expensive to buy
- Only showerproof. You'll have to use a waterproof oversuit in wet weather
- Not warm. Due to the close fit, you can't wear extra layers underneath in cold weather
- There can be some restriction of movement

Two-piece zip-together suits

These comprise a separate jacket and trousers which zip together. This style has some advantages

- You can buy the jacket or trousers separately. This lets you spread the cost to suit your budget. It also lets you buy different sizes to suit you
- Zipping the jacket and trousers together helps to stop draughts around your waist
- Jacket or trousers can be worn separately

Separate jacket and trousers

This option

- Is often the least expensive
- Gives you a wide choice of styles, colours, sizes and prices

When you are choosing leathers look for additional protection for shoulders, elbows and knees.

Visit your motorcycle dealer or motorcycle clothing supplier. Try on various types of clothing for fit and comfort. As a general rule, buy the best you can afford.

Gloves and gauntlets

Good gloves or gauntlets are essential items when you ride a motorcycle. Never be tempted to ride without gloves. If you fall off you could seriously injure your hands. Your gloves should

- Protect your hands from cold and wet weather
- Protect your hands if you fall off
- Allow you to operate the controls easily

Gauntlets prevent wind and rain from being driven up your sleeves. However, in heavy rain the water can sometimes run down your sleeves into your gloves. Modern motorcycle gauntlets have adjustable cuffs to help overcome this problem.

Materials

Leather is the most suitable material for motorcycle gloves. It's tough, supple and resistant to water. It's also expensive. Gloves made from cheaper materials don't provide the same level of protection. For protection from prolonged rain you'll need to wear overmitts.

Overmitts

Overmitts prevent gloves from becoming sodden in prolonged wet-weather riding. You wear them over your usual motorcycle gloves or gauntlets. They are made from waterproof material, either waxed cotton or nylon. Make sure that you can operate the controls properly when wearing overmitts.

Cold

When riding in very cold weather your hands can become painfully cold. No matter how good your gloves the cold will eventually get through. This in turn can cause you to lose concentration when riding.

To overcome the cold you can try wearing thin inner gloves. Experiment with various combinations to find one that suits you.

Heated gloves and handlebar grips

If you're serious about motorcycling in cold weather then you'll need either

- Electrically heated inner gloves
- Electrically heated handlebar grips

These accessories put a large demand on your motorcycle's electrical generator. Check that it can cope with the extra demands before you buy and fit them.

Boots

It's important to wear good boots or stout footwear when you ride a motorcycle. If you wear sandals or trainers your feet will have little protection if you fall off.

Motorcycle boots

- Protect your feet from cold and wet weather
- Offer some protection if you have an accident
- Protect your feet and shins from knocks and bumps

Types of boots

There are two types of motorcycle boots

- Leather
- Rubber or plastic

Leather boots Leather is strong, flexible and weather resistant. This makes it the most suitable material for motorcycle boots. Leather boots give the best protection in the event of an accident.

As leather isn't totally waterproof you might need overboots in very wet weather.

Leather boots are available either unlined or lined with warm fleece material.

Rubber or plastic boots Rubber or plastic boots are

- Waterproof
- Cheaper than leather

You can buy them lined or unlined, and leather-look boots are also available.

Whichever type of boot you decide to buy make sure that

- They're comfortable
- You can operate the foot controls easily

Try as many different boots as you can. Always buy the best you can afford.

Cold

Your feet can become very cold when you're riding in wintry conditions. Wearing an extra pair of socks can help. If your feet become too cold stop and warm up before continuing your journey.

Fluorescent jacket

In daylight

Wearing fluorescent orange or yellow clothing will improve your chances of being seen. This can be

- A fluorescent jacket
- A fluorescent tabard or waistcoat
- A 'Sam Browne' belt

You need to be visible from the side as well as the front and back.

Other methods you could use to help other road users to see you in daylight include

- Wearing a white helmet
- Wearing bright-coloured clothing
- Riding with your headlamp on dipped beam

Visibility aids

Many road accidents involving motorcyclists occur because another road user didn't see them. Using some form of visibility aid will help others to see you.

DSA THE MOTORCYCLING MANUAL

In the dark

To improve visibility in the dark you need to wear reflective material. This can be reflective

- Belts
- Patches
- Strips

They work by reflecting the light from headlamps of other vehicles. This makes you much more visible from a long distance away.

Reflective strips on your gloves will help other road users to see your arm signals.

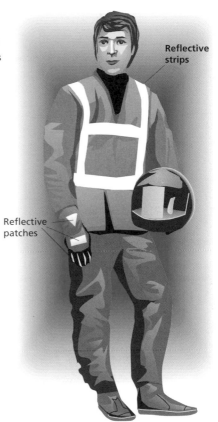

Reflective strips

Reflective patches

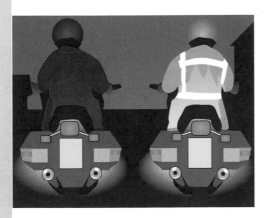

Safety helmets

By law, you must wear a safety helmet when riding a motorcycle on the road. (Members of the Sikh religion who wear a turban are exempt.)

All helmets sold in the UK must

- Carry a BSI kitemark
- Comply with British Standard BS 6658

Types of safety helmet

Motorcycle helmets are either

- Full-face
- Open-face

Full-face helmets This type of helmet

- Covers the head fully and has a hinged visor
- Protects the face in an accident
- Offers more weather protection than an open-face helmet

Open-face helmets This type of helmet

- Is preferred by riders who feel closed in by full-face helmets
- Can be worn with either a visor or goggles
- Doesn't protect the chin in an accident

Whichever type of helmet you choose, you must make sure that it

- Fits properly
- Is correctly fastened

Helmet fit

When you buy a new helmet make sure that it's a good, firm fit. The padding will soon bed down and this could make the helmet loose. A loose helmet isn't only uncomfortable, it could also come off in an accident.

Helmet fastening

There are three different helmet fastening methods in use today. The three different methods are illustrated.

Some helmet straps also have a velcro tab. This is to secure the strap so that it doesn't flap in the wind. It **isn't** to be used to fasten the helmet.

It is both unsafe and illegal to ride in a helmet which isn't

- Fastened correctly
- Fastened at all

Double D ring

Quick release

Bar and buckle

Helmet materials

Motorcycle safety helmets are made in three basic materials

- Polycarbonate
- Glass fibre
- Kevlar

Each material has its own characteristics.

Polycarbonate

- Lighter than glass fibre
- Must not be painted or have stickers affixed
- Must not be cleaned with solvents

Polycarbonate helmets tend to be cheaper than other types and don't last as long.

Glass fibre

- Heavier than polycarbonate
- Last longer than polycarbonate
- Easy to clean

Kevlar   An extremely tough material which

- Is used as a composite with glass fibre, or carbon and glass fibre
- Combines great strength with light weight
- Tends to be expensive

Damage to helmets

If your helmet receives any serious impact buy a new one. Damage won't always be visible to the naked eye. For this reason never use a second-hand helmet. A damaged helmet could be unreliable in an accident. Some helmets can be professionally repaired by the manufacturer. Your motorcycle equipment dealer should be able to advise you further.

Visors and goggles

A visor or goggles are vital to protect your eyes from wind, rain, insects and road dirt.

All visors and goggles must

- Comply with British Standard
  - BS 4110 XA or
  - BS 4110 YA or
  - BS 4110 ZA
- Display a BSI kitemark

Glasses and tinted eyewear

If you normally wear glasses or contact lenses you must by law wear them when you ride.

Don't wear tinted glasses, visors or goggles if you're riding in

- The dark
- Conditions of poor visibility

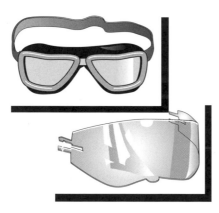

Cleaning your visor or goggles

It's very important that you keep your visor or goggles clean. You must have a clear view of the road ahead at all times.

To clean your goggles or visor wash them in warm soapy water. Don't use solvents or petrol.

In cold and wet weather your visor or goggles might fog up on the inside. You can use a special anti-fog spray to help prevent this. If your visor or goggles fog up when you're riding

- Choose somewhere safe to stop
- Wipe them with a clean damp cloth. Carry a cloth with you for this purpose

Damaged or scratched goggles and visors

Scratches on your visor or goggles can

- Distort your view
- Cause dazzle from the lights of oncoming vehicles at night
- Cause glare, especially from the low winter sun

If your visor or goggles are heavily scratched renew them

Motorcycle fairings

Motorcycle fairings come in three main types

- Touring fairings
- Sports fairings
- Handlebar fairings

Handlebar fairings

These protect your hands and body and are available in either sports or touring styles.

Touring fairings

These provide weather protection to the hands, legs and feet. They also make high-speed riding more comfortable by keeping you out of the wind.

Sports fairings

These give some weather protection but they're mainly intended to cut down wind resistance

Windscreens

These protect your face and body
from the wind and rain.

Handlebar muffs

Handlebar muffs are designed to
keep the wind and rain off your
hands.

Motorcycles have various types of controls. Before you learn to ride you should become familar with their position, function and use.

Most motorcycles have the controls in similar positions but there are some important differences. For example, most motorcycles have manual transmission but some have automatic and others semi-automatic.

This part is a general guide to the controls on a typical motorcycle.

The topics covered

- Typical position of controls
- Foot controls
- Left handlebar controls
- Right handlebar controls
- Mirrors
- Instrument panel

Typical position of motorcycle controls

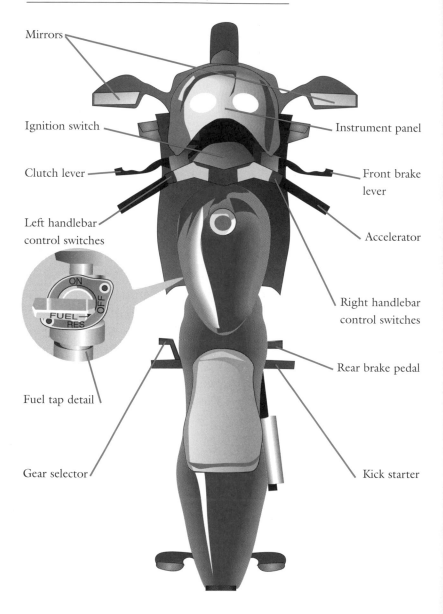

Mirrors

Ignition switch

Clutch lever

Left handlebar
control switches

Fuel tap detail

Gear selector

Instrument panel

Front brake
lever

Accelerator

Right handlebar
control switches

Rear brake pedal

Kick starter

Foot controls

Gear selector

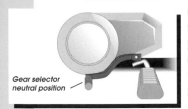

Gear selector
neutral position

Gears enable you to match engine power to road speed. Low gears allow the engine power to be used at lower road speeds. Use these when you're moving off, going uphill or accelerating. High gears allow the same engine power to be used at higher road speeds.

Changing smoothly through the gears is a skill that will improve with practice.

Position The gear selector is usually on the left side of the motorcycle. It's just in front of the footrest.

Some mopeds and scooters have a twist-grip gear change on the left handlebar.

Neutral The neutral position is when no gear is engaged. Most motorcycles have a green warning lamp to show when the gears are in neutral.

To select gears On motorcycles the gears are selected by lifting or pushing down the gear lever with your foot. The positions and number of gears vary with the make of motorcycle.

Rear brake pedal

This applies the brake to the rear wheel.

Position This pedal is usually on the right side of the motorcycle, just in front of the footrest. Some automatic motorcycles have the rear brake lever on the left handlebar.

Use To apply the brake press the pedal with your foot. To release the brake release the pedal.

Kick-start lever

Position This lever is usually found on the right side of the motorcycle, near the footrest.

Use

- Make sure that the cut-out switch is on
- Switch on the ignition
- Put the gear selector in neutral and check that the neutral lamp glows
- Fold out the kick-start lever. (You may need to fold the footrest out of the way.)
- Tread down sharply on the lever. Repeat this until the engine starts

Left handlebar controls

HEADLAMP DIP SWITCH

This switch lets you switch your headlamp between main beam and dipped beam.

On main beam you'll usually see a blue warning lamp on your instruments. At night, switch to dipped beam when meeting or following other vehicles. This will stop you dazzling other drivers.

HEADLAMP FLASHER

This switch lets you flash your headlamp. This has the same meaning as sounding your horn. Flash your headlamp if your horn may not be heard, for example on the motorway.

CLUTCH LEVER

CHOKE

HORN

Sound the horn to warn other road users if you don't think they've seen you.

You must not sound your horn

• Between 11.30 pm and 7 am in a built-up area

• When your motorcycle is stationary, unless a moving vehicle poses a danger

INDICATORS

You use the indicators to let other road users know that you intend to change direction. You must make sure that you cancel them after turning.

CLUTCH LEVER

This lever operates the clutch, which engages and disengages the engine from the rear wheel.

Use the clutch

- When you select first gear before moving off
- To prevent the engine stalling when you stop
- To help change gears
- When selecting neutral

To change or select a gear

- Pull the clutch lever fully to the handlebar
- Select the gear you need
- Release the clutch lever smoothly to engage the clutch

Fully automatic motorcycles This type of motorcycle has no clutch lever. You select drive or neutral as required. Often the rear brake lever is fitted in place of the clutch lever.

Semi-automatic motorcycles These have no clutch lever. The clutch operates automatically when you use the gear-change pedal.

CHOKE

The choke is a device which helps when starting a cold engine. It operates by changing the amount of air in the air/fuel mixture which the engine burns.

When you're starting a cold engine

- Move the choke control to 'on'
- Start the engine
- Gradually move the choke control to 'off' as the engine warms up

Note Failure to return the choke to 'off' could cause the engine to run faster than normal. This could make it difficult to control the motorcycle, especially when slowing down. In addition it could cause excessive wear to the engine and excessive fuel consumption.

Right handlebar controls

ENGINE CUT-OUT SWITCH

This is to stop the engine in an emergency. It shuts off all electrical circuits, so reducing fire hazard in an accident.

When stopping the engine normally, use the ignition switch. You're less likely to leave your keys in the ignition when leaving your motorcycle.

ELECTRIC STARTER

This is fitted as well as, or in place of, the kick starter.

Use

• Check the cut-out switch is on

• Switch the ignition on

• Make sure that the gear selector is in neutral

• Press the starter button

LIGHT SWITCH

This is a three-position switch letting you select

- Headlights
- Parking lights
- Off

FRONT BRAKE LEVER

This lever applies the brake to the front wheel.

To apply the front brake squeeze the lever toward you. Use all the fingers on your right hand for maximum control and stopping power. The harder you squeeze, the harder you brake. To release the brake release the lever.

ACCELERATOR (THROTTLE)

The throttle controls the engine speed. It increases or decreases the amount of fuel delivered to the engine.

To speed up the engine twist the throttle towards you. To slow down the engine twist the grip away from you. Most throttles will spring back to a closed position when released. In this position the engine should run at 'idle' or 'tick over' speed.

Mirrors

Mirrors are fitted to both right and left handlebars, or sometimes on the fairing.

Mirrors should be adjusted to give you the best view of the road behind. However, your elbows may obscure the view behind. If they do, try fitting alternative mirrors with longer stems.

There are two types of mirror available

- Flat mirrors. These don't distort the picture of the road behind. This makes it easier for you to judge the speed and distance of following traffic

- Convex mirrors. These are slightly curved and give a wider field of vision. This makes it more difficult to judge the speed and distance of following traffic

Instrument panel

Speedometer

The speedometer tells you how fast you're going in miles per hour and kilometres per hour.

Mileometer (odometer)

This is usually housed in the speedometer. It shows an overall total of how many miles your motorcycle has covered.

Temperature gauge

This is fitted to motorcycles with liquid-cooled engines. It shows the coolant temperature and warns if the engine is overheating.

Rev. counter

This shows the engine speed in revolutions per minute.

Indicator repeater

This tells you that your indicators are in use. Use it to check if you've cancelled a signal.

Ignition lamp

This lamp comes on when you switch on the ignition. It should go out when the engine is running. If it doesn't this shows a problem with the battery-charging system.

Ignition switch

This switch is operated by the ignition key. There are three main positions

- Off
- On
- Lock. In this position the steering locks to help prevent theft

Neutral lamp

This lamp glows to tell you when the gear selector is in the neutral position.

High beam lamp

This indicates when your headlamp is on high beam.

Oil pressure lamp

This lamp warns you of low oil pressure. If it comes on when the engine is running you may have a serious problem. Stop the engine immediately and investigate the cause.

Compulsory Basic Training (CBT) was introduced in 1990 to help reduce the very high accident rate among inexperienced motorcyclists. This accident rate has since fallen significantly, perhaps indicating that properly trained motorcyclists are safer motorcyclists.

CBT can only be given by Approved Training Bodies (ATBs) and provides training in a safe environment. Don't be put off motorcycling because of CBT. Many people find it an enjoyable learning experience. Taking CBT will give your motorcycling career the right start.

The topics covered

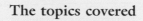

- **Introduction to CBT**

- **Element A: Introduction**

- **Element B: Practical on-site training**

- **Element C: Practical on-site riding**

- **Element D: Practical on-road training**

- **Element E: Practical on-road riding**

- **The Certificate of Completion**

Introduction to CBT

Before you ride on the road you must satisfactorily complete a CBT course, unless you hold a licence with provisional motorcycle entitlement which started before 1 December 1990. From 1 January 1997 the law changes and all learner motorcycle and moped riders must satisfactorily complete CBT before riding on the road. (See Part Two for special exemptions.)

The CBT course covers five elements. These have to be taken **in sequence.**

When you've satisfactorily completed all five elements you'll be issued with a Certificate of Completion of training (DL196).

Approved Training Bodies (ATBs) run CBT courses. ATBs have

- Instructors who have passed the Driving Standards Agency (DSA) course
- Sites approved by the DSA for off-road training

Training organisations

You can find out about CBT courses in your area from

- Your local Road Safety Officer
- Your motorcycle dealer
- Motorcycle papers and magazines
- Local *Yellow Pages*
- The DSA
  Tel: 0115 955 7600

Element A: Introduction

Before you do any practical training you must understand

- The aims of the CBT course
- The importance of the right equipment and clothing
- The need to be clearly visible to other road users
- The legal requirements when riding on the road
- Why motorcyclists are more vulnerable than other road users
- The need to ride at the correct speed according to road and traffic conditions
- The importance of reading and understanding *The Highway Code*

Eyesight

Your eyesight will be tested and you must be able to read a number plate

- In good daylight
- Containing letters and figures 79.4 mm (3.1 in) high
- At a distance of 20.5 metres (about 67 feet)
- With the aid of glasses or contact lenses if you normally wear them

Element B:
Practical on-site training

This element provides you with an introduction to your motorcycle. At the end of this element you'll have demonstrated that

- You're familiar with the motorcycle, its controls and how it works
- You're able to carry out basic machine checks
- You're able to take the motorcycle on and off its stand
- You're able to wheel the motorcycle around to the left and right, showing proper balance
- You're able to bring the motorcycle to a halt by braking
- You can start and stop the engine satisfactorily

Element C:
Practical on-site riding

In this element you start to ride your motorcycle. You'll practise until you can demonstrate your ability to

- Ride your motorcycle under control in a straight line, and bring it to a controlled halt
- Ride your motorcycle slowly under control
- Carry out controlled braking using both brakes
- Bring your motorcycle to a controlled stop, as in an emergency
- Change gear satisfactorily

- Ride your motorcycle in a figure-of-eight circuit
- Carry out rear observations correctly
- Carry out simulated left and right turns correctly using the Observation – Signal – Manoeuvre (OSM) routine and the Position – Speed – Look (PSL) routine

The OSM – PSL routine is explained later in this book.

Element D:
Practical on-road training

This element will take place as some form of discussion with your instructor. Before you venture onto the road you must understand the need to

- Ride defensively and to anticipate the actions of other road users

- Use rear observation at appropriate times

- Assume the correct road position when riding

- Leave sufficient space when following another vehicle

- Pay due regard to the effect of varying weather conditions when riding

- Be aware of the various types of road surfaces and how to cope with them

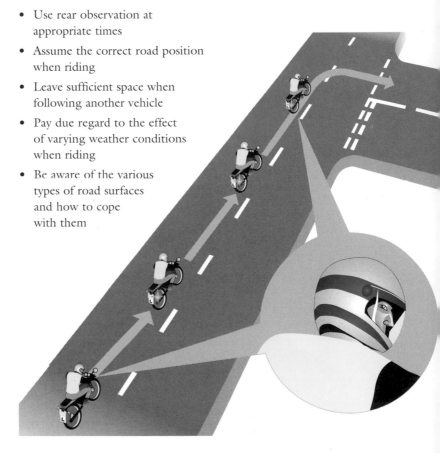

Element E:
Practical on-road riding

For this final element you'll go out on the road with your instructor for a minimum of two hours, possibly with another trainee. You'll have to demonstrate that you can ride competently and safely in a variety of road and traffic conditions. Your training will cover how to cope with a range of hazards and include as many of the following as possible

- Traffic lights
- Roundabouts
- Junctions
- Pedestrian crossings
- Gradients
- Bends
- Obstructions

The Certificate of Completion

When you've satisfactorily completed Element E you'll be given a Certificate of Completion of the approved training course (DL196). This certificate validates the provisional motorcycle entitlement on your driving licence.

With the DL196 you're now licensed to ride on the road and to practise for your motorcycle or moped test. Talk to your Approved Training Body about taking further training to prepare for the test.

When you apply for a motorcycle or moped test either

- Send the DL196 with your application
- Present it to your driving examiner when you attend the test

It's important that you remember this otherwise your test will be cancelled and you'll lose your fee.

Certificate life

CBT certificates have a three-year life. This includes

- Certificates issued before 1 July 1996, which will have a three-year life from that date
- Certificates issued on or after 1 July 1996. These will have a three-year life from their date of issue

This part takes you through the basics of motorcycle handling and control. When you take CBT the topics will be covered in the earlier Elements. (see Part Six).

If you're allowed to ride a moped without L plates you aren't required to take CBT. But if you've never ridden a moped or motorcycle you're strongly advised to do so before riding on the road.

The topics covered

- Stands
- Mounting and dismounting
- Riding position
- Starting the engine
- Stopping the engine
- Moving off
- Stopping
- Practice

Stands

When you park a motorcycle you use a stand to support it. Motorcycles have either a centre or side stand, and many models are fitted with both.

Centre stand

The centre stand gives more stable support than the side stand. It also supports the motorcycle so that maintenance can be carried out such as

- Drive chain adjustment (where fitted)
- Wheel removal

The centre stand needs to be used on a firm, level surface for maximum stability.

To put your motorcycle onto the centre stand

- Position yourself on the left of the motorcycle, holding the left handlebar with the left hand
- Push the stand down with your right foot (left foot, if preferred) and hold the frame near the saddle with your right hand. (Some machines have a special grab handle.)
- Hold the stand down with your foot and pull the machine backwards and upwards

To take your motorcycle off the centre stand

- Position yourself on the left of the motorcycle. Put your left foot (right, if preferred) in front of the centre stand
- Hold the left handlebar with your left hand. Hold the frame near the saddle with your right hand
- Pull the motorcycle forward. As it comes off the stand move your right hand to the front brake to keep control

Warning If the stand isn't fully up it could dig into the road when you're cornering and cause an accident.

Side stand

The side stand is generally quicker and easier to use than the centre stand. It relies on the motorcycle leaning over onto the stand for stability.

Care must be taken to ensure that the

- Surface is firm enough to prevent the side stand sinking and the motorcycle falling over
- Slope of the ground doesn't prevent the motorcycle leaning onto the stand. If the machine is too upright it will be unstable

To put your motorcycle onto the side stand

- Position yourself on the left of the machine, holding the left handlebar
- With the machine upright, push down the stand with your right foot (left, if preferred)
- Let the machine lean towards you until its weight is taken on the stand

To take your motorcycle off the side stand

- Position yourself on the left of the machine holding the handlebars
- Push the motorcycle upright
- Move the stand to its up position with your foot. Make sure it locks securely in position

Warning   If the stand isn't fully up it could dig into the road when you're cornering and cause an accident. Some machines have an inhibitor switch which will automatically stop the engine if you try to ride off with the side stand down.

Mounting and dismounting

Always mount from the left of the motorcycle, the side away from the traffic. As you get on or off apply the front brake to stop the motorcycle moving.

Practise mounting and dismounting with the motorcycle off its stand.

Balancing and wheeling your motorcycle

After you've practised mounting and dismounting, wheel the machine forward. Leaning the motorcycle towards you makes it easier to balance.

Work the front brake with your right hand to control the speed.

Practise wheeling the machine in circles, both to the left and to the right. Keep practising until you're able to balance and control it fully.

Adjusting the controls

You can adjust the main motorcycle controls to suit your individual needs. If you can't use them comfortably and safely when you're riding adjust the

- Hand controls, such as front brake and clutch levers
- Foot controls, such as the footbrake and gear selector

Riding position

When you're seated on a stationary motorcycle you should be able to

- Place both feet on the ground
- Use one foot to keep your balance and the other to work the foot controls

The best posture

Sit in a natural position, as determined by the machine design. You should be able to reach all the controls comfortably.

Starting the engine

Some engines can require a knack to make them start. The following is a general guide, but you may need to modify it to suit your machine.

To start the engine

- Make sure that the gear selector is in neutral. The neutral lamp on the instument panel will glow when the ignition is turned on. If no neutral lamp is fitted push your motorcycle forward to see if the rear wheel turns freely
- Turn the fuel tap to 'on'
- If the engine is cold move the choke to 'on'
- Make sure that the engine cut-out switch is in the 'on' position
- Turn the ignition key to the 'on' position

Your motorcycle is now ready to start. The next step depends on whether your machine has an electric starter or a kick starter.

Electric starter

- Press the starter button
- Open the throttle to give a fairly high engine speed
- As the engine warms up move the choke to 'off'

Kick starter

- Fold out the kick-start lever. On some machines you'll have to fold the footrest up before you can use the kick starter
- Place your instep on the lever and tread down sharply. Allow the kick-start lever to return to its upright position. Repeat this until the engine starts
- When the engine has started, fold the kick-start lever back to its resting position
- Open the throttle to give a fairly high engine speed
- As the engine warms up move the choke to 'off'

Stopping the engine

This safe sequence applies to most motorcycles

- Close the throttle fully
- Make sure that the gear selector is in neutral
- Switch the ignition key to 'off'. Take out the key in the Lock position if you're leaving your machine
- Turn the fuel tap to 'off', unless it's vacuum-operated

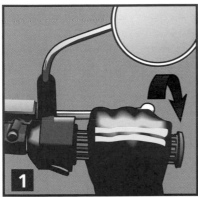

Moving off

You'll learn to move off during CBT and will be taught in a suitable place off the public road.

To move off, follow these steps in order

- Sit astride your machine
- Apply the front brake and then start the engine
- Squeeze in the clutch lever. Use all your fingers to get full control
- Select first gear. Keep the clutch lever held in
- Put your left foot on the ground and shift the weight of the machine to that foot. Put your right foot on the footrest and then apply the rear brake

You can now release the front brake and work the throttle.

- Release the clutch lever smoothly, until you feel the engine trying to move the machine. This is called the 'biting point'. Open the throttle enough to keep the engine running smoothly

You're now ready to move off.

- Gradually release the clutch lever and at the same time open the throttle smoothly. As you move off release the rear brake and bring your left foot up onto the footrest

Clutch control

Smooth clutch control is essential to good riding. It's also one of the most difficult skills for the novice to acquire.

You must be able to find the biting point easily when releasing the clutch lever. This skill will develop with practice.

Balance

When you're manoeuvring a motorcycle the weight may make it awkward to handle. When you're riding, however, you should find the weight improves the stability and balance.

Never look down at the front wheel when riding – this can severely upset your balance.

Stopping

Having learnt how to move off you also need to learn how to stop. The following sequence will apply to most motorcycles

- Close the throttle
- Apply both brakes smoothly until the machine stops
- Just before the motorcycle stops pull in the clutch lever to avoid stalling the engine
- As the machine stops put your left foot on the ground to support the weight

When the machine has stopped

- Keep the front brake applied
- Release the rear brake and support the motorcycle with your right foot

With the clutch lever still pulled in

- Use your left foot to move the gear selector to neutral
- Release the clutch lever
- Place both feet on the ground

Disengaging the clutch

When stopping from very low speeds pull in the clutch lever *just before* or *just as* you brake.

When stopping from higher road speeds always brake first, then pull in the clutch lever just before you stop.

Practice

You'll need to practise these basic skills. Choose a suitable place off the public road where you won't cause any danger or nuisance to anyone. You should practise

- Starting and stopping when riding in a straight line
- Riding in circles to the left and right, making the circles gradually smaller
- Riding slowly until you can turn, start and stop with confidence

You need to practise turning to the left and right with both feet on the footrests.

You must also be able to work the clutch and throttle together, and to brake safely.

Having learnt the basics of motorcycle control you can venture out onto the road. First learn to handle your motorcycle on quiet roads. Try to stay away from more demanding road and traffic conditions until you've gained confidence.

This part deals with putting your training into practice on the road.

The topics covered

- **Moving off safely**
- **Stopping safely**
- **Using the gears**
- **Using the brakes**
- **The road surface**
- **Emergency braking**
- **Skidding**
- **Stopping distance**
- **Parking**

Moving off safely

To move off safely on the road you have to think about other road users. Can you move off without endangering yourself or anyone else? To answer this question you need to have a good look around.

Having got your machine ready to move off, look round over your right shoulder (unless you're on the right-hand side of the road) and then look ahead. You're looking to make sure that

- There's no traffic approaching from behind
- The way ahead is clear
- You're safe to move off

Look out for pedestrians and cyclists – they're harder to see than cars.

You should signal if it will help any other road user.

Important   It's very important that you look round before moving off, even if you have mirrors fitted. Looking round will allow you to

- Accurately judge how far away any traffic may be, and how fast it's travelling

- See if there's anything in the blind area on your right. The blind area is the area behind and to your right which isn't covered by mirrors (see Part Nine)

Stopping safely

To stop safely you need to make sure that you don't endanger any other road users. You should

- Use your mirrors and look over your right shoulder, if necessary, to check for following traffic
- Signal if it will help other road users. People in front may benefit from a signal just as much as people behind

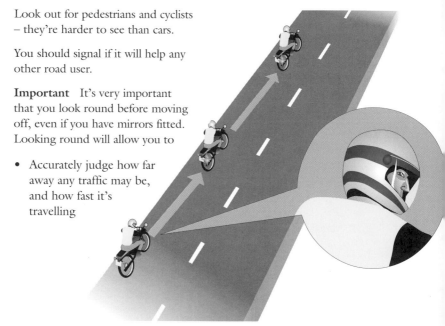

DSA THE MOTORCYCLING MANUAL

Using the gears

Gear changing

To change up or down through the gears you need to be able to co-ordinate the

- Clutch
- Throttle
- Gear selector

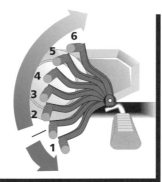

Gear selector neutral and return position

Changing up   Change gear when you've reached the appropriate speed for the next gear

- Simultaneously close the throttle and pull in the clutch lever
- Select the next higher gear by lifting the gear selector with the toe of your boot. Allow the selector to return to its normal position after each change
- Release the clutch lever smoothly and open the throttle at the same time
- Repeat the sequence for each upward gear change

Always travel in the highest suitable gear. You'll save fuel and spare your engine.

Changing down

- Simultaneously close the throttle and pull in the clutch lever
- Select the next lower gear by pushing down the gear selector with the toe of your boot. Allow the selector to return to its normal position after each gear change
- At the same time, release the clutch lever smoothly and open the throttle as necessary

When to change

Experience will tell you when to change gear. You'll be able to hear from the engine sound when a gear change is needed. Never let the engine

- Race when you could change to a higher gear
- Labour when you could change to a lower gear

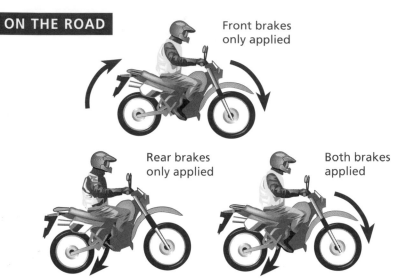

Front brakes only applied

Rear brakes only applied

Both brakes applied

Using the brakes

How to brake

Many motorcycle riders are, quite wrongly, afraid to use the front brake. This is often as a result of what they were taught as cyclists. On a motorcycle

- You must normally use both brakes
- The front brake is the more powerful of the two brakes and the most important when stopping a motorcycle

To stop most effectively   In good road and weather conditions

- Apply the front brake a fraction of a second before you apply the rear brake
- Apply greater pressure to the front brake

Applying greater pressure to the front brake gives the best stopping power in good conditions because

- The combined weight of the machine and rider is thrown forward
- The front tyre is pressed more firmly on the road, giving a better grip

In wet or slippery conditions you need to apply a more equal pressure to both front and rear brakes.

Using one brake only   You'll take much longer to stop by using one brake only. But at very low speeds (walking pace) using only the rear brake gives smoother control.

When to brake

Always look and plan well ahead to avoid having to brake sharply. A gradual increase of pressure on the brakes is better than late, harsh braking.

Follow these rules

- Brake when your machine is upright and moving in a straight line
- Brake in good time
- Adjust the pressure on the brakes according to the road surface and weather conditions

Where to brake

Where you brake is very important. The best time to brake is when you're travelling

- Upright
- In a straight line

Braking in a bend A good rider will plan well ahead to avoid braking in a bend. In a bend the combined weight of motorcycle and rider is thrown outwards. To balance this the rider leans inwards slightly.

If you brake in a bend

- The weight will be thrown outwards even more
- The motorcycle and rider may become unstable
- The tyres may lose their grip on the road surface

If you must brake in a bend

- Avoid using the front brake. Rely on the rear brake and engine braking to slow you down. If you must use the front brake, be very gentle. There's a risk of the front tyre losing its grip and sliding sideways
- Try to bring your motorcycle upright and brake normally (provided you can do so safely)

The road surface

The state of the road surface is very important to motorcyclists. Only a small part of the motorcycle tyre makes contact with the road. Any change in the surface can therefore affect the stability of your motorcycle.

Be on the lookout for poor road surfaces. Look out for

- Loose surfaces, such as chippings, gravel, mud and leaves
- Pot-holes and uneven surfaces
- Inspection covers, especially when wet
- Oil patches, especially at roundabouts, bus stops and filling stations
- Tar banding around road repairs
- Painted road markings

- Rails set into the road for Supertrams or Light Rapid Transit systems. These can affect your steering and present a hazard when braking
- Any shiny road surface. At junctions, frequent braking and acceleration can polish the surface

If you can safely avoid riding on slippery surfaces then do so. If you have to ride on a slippery surface slow down well in advance. Don't swerve suddenly to avoid a poor surface.

If you find yourself on a slippery surface check the traffic, then gradually slow down.

Part Twelve, Riding in Bad Weather, contains information on the effects of weather on the road surface.

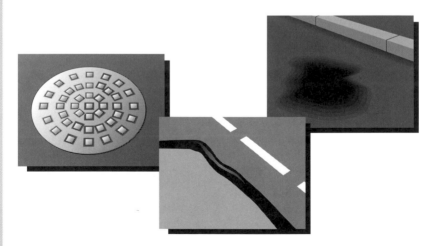

Emergency braking

If you plan ahead you should seldom need to brake violently or stop suddenly. Nevertheless, emergencies do arise and you must be able to stop safely and quickly.

Maximum braking

- Use the front brake just before the rear
- Brake progressively (increase pressure steadily)
- Apply the right amount of braking effort to each wheel. This will depend on the road surface and weather conditions

Braking in an emergency

- Keep your motorcycle upright
- Apply maximum effort without locking the wheels. This is achieved by progressively increasing braking pressure. Don't use the brakes violently – this may cause you to skid

- Pull in the clutch lever just before you stop

Signalling when you brake

Don't try to give an arm signal when you brake in an emergency

- You'll need both hands on the handlebars
- Your stop lamp will warn traffic behind you

Rear brakes only

Front brakes only

Both brakes applied (front first)

These three bikes were travelling at 40 mph before braking together

Skidding

A skid is when tyres

- Lose their grip on the road surface
- Veer off the steered course
- Reduce the effect of the brakes (by sliding over the road surface)

Causes of skidding

- Heavy or unco-ordinated braking, which locks one or both wheels
- Excessive acceleration, causing the driven wheel to spin
- Swerving (a sudden change of direction)
- Leaning over too far when cornering, causing one or both tyres to lose grip

A good rider tries to avoid skidding. The loss of control which can arise from a skid can be lethal.

Heavy braking

Wheelspin (severe acceleration)

Swerving (changing direction suddenly)

Leaning too far over when cornering

Dealing with skids

Skids can happen suddenly.
You need to know how to regain
control when skidding occurs.

Excessive acceleration If you've
caused a skid by excessive
acceleration

- The rear wheelspin can cause
  your machine to slide sideways.
  Steer in the direction that your
  machine is sliding

- Ease off the throttle to regain
  control

Braking If you've caused a skid by
braking

- Ease off the brakes to let the
  wheels start turning again

- Re-apply the brakes as firmly
  as the conditions will permit

Your natural instincts when dealing
with a brake skid will be to brake
even harder. You must learn to
overcome such instincts if you're
to regain control.

Correcting a skid

- Steer into the skid. If the
  machine is sliding to the right,
  steer to the right. If the machine
  is sliding to the left, steer to the
  left

- Keep your feet on the footrests.
  Putting your feet to the ground
  on a moving motorcycle could
  upset your balance

Skids are a lot easier to get into than
they are to get out of. Remember,
skid control is an emergency measure
– it's no substitute for skid avoidance.

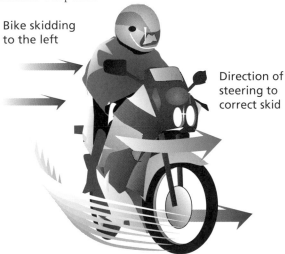

Bike skidding
to the left

Direction of
steering to
correct skid

- Ease off brake
- Steer to left

Stopping distance

It's important for you to know the stopping distance at all speeds. This is the distance your motorcycle travels

- From the moment you realise you must brake
- To the moment your machine stops

Always ride so that you can stop safely within the distance you can see to be clear.

Stopping distance depends on

- How fast you're going
- Whether you're travelling uphill, on the level or downhill
- The weather and the state of the road
- The condition of your brakes and tyres
- Your ability, especially your reaction times

Stopping distance divides into

- Thinking distance
- Braking distance

Thinking distance

'Thinking distance' is from the point where you see the hazard to the point where you brake. This distance will vary from rider to rider and is dependent upon reaction time. Reaction times are affected by

- Age
- Physical and mental condition
- Health
- Time of day
- Alcohol or drugs

An alert and fit rider needs 0.75 of a second thinking time. That means that at 50 mph you'll travel 15 metres (about 50 feet) **before you begin to brake.**

At 30 mph

Thinking distance	Braking distance	Overall stopping distance
9 metres (30 feet)	14 metres (45 feet)	23 metres (75 feet)

At 50 mph

Thinking distance	Braking distance	Overall stopping distance
15 metres (50 feet)	38 metres (125 feet)	53 metres (175 feet)

At 70 mph

Thinking distance	Braking distance	Overall stopping distance
21 metres (70 feet)	75 metres (245 feet)	96 metres (315 feet)

Braking distance

'Braking distance' is from the point where you begin to brake to the point where you stop.

Braking distance depends upon

- Road conditions
- Tyre condition
- Brake efficiency
- Suspension efficiency
- Load. It takes longer to stop if you're carrying a passenger
- Rider ability

Most of all, braking distance varies with speed. At 30 mph your braking distance will be 14 metres (about 45 feet) while at 70 mph that distance will increase to 75 metres (about 245 feet). That's just over double the speed but more than **five times** the braking distance.

Overall stopping distance   Your overall stopping distance also increases dramatically as you increase your road speed. The scale of the stopping distance as it changes with speed is illustrated.

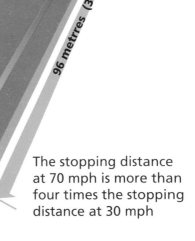

23 metres (75 feet)

96 metres (315 feet)

The stopping distance at 70 mph is more than four times the stopping distance at 30 mph

Parking

The parking rules in *The Highway Code* also apply to motorcycles. When you park, take care to

- Park on firm, level ground. On soft ground the stand can sink, causing the machine to fall over. On a very hot day side or centre stands can sink into tarmac softened by the heat. If your machine falls over it could injure a passer-by or damage another parked vehicle

- Use the centre stand if you're leaving your machine for some time

- Switch off the fuel tap

- Secure your motorcycle using the steering lock and/or use a purpose-made motorcycle lock

- Take the ignition key with you

If you park a side-car outfit on a gradient make sure that it doesn't roll away. Leave the machine in a low gear and block a wheel or wedge it against the kerb.

Motorcycle parking places

In many towns you can find areas set aside for motorcycle parking. Some car parks also set aside areas for motorcycles. Look for signs or marked-out parking bays.

MOTORCYCLE
PARKING

Wherever you ride you're going to have to deal with traffic. Traffic volumes vary from heavily congested urban roads to light traffic on rural roads. You need to know how to cope safely with the problems modern-day traffic presents.

This part outlines the problems of riding in traffic and the techniques you need to learn to ride safely.

The topics covered

- Signals
- Looking behind
- Mirrors
- Road position
- Road junctions
- Emerging

Signals

You need to give signals to

- Help other road users, including pedestrians
- Let other road users know what you intend to do

Road users include

- Drivers of following and oncoming vehicles
- Cyclists
- Pedestrians
- Traffic controllers
- Police directing traffic

Always signal **clearly** and in **good time.** Give only correct signals, as shown.

Arm signals

Arm signals are very effective in daylight especially when you're wearing bright or fluorescent clothing.

Giving an arm signal means that you have reduced steering control, if only briefly. Spend some time practising controlling your motorcycle while giving arm signals.

Practise

- With one hand and then with the other
- Before you ride on the road

Give arm signals in good time. Don't try to keep up the signal all the way through a turn. You'll need both hands on the handlebars to make any turn safely.

I intend to move out to the right or turn right

I intend to move in to the left or turn left

I intend to slow down or to stop

Signals to traffic controllers

I want to turn right

I want to turn left

I want to go straight on

Arm signals at speed When travelling at speed on the open road, arm signals can upset your stability. At speed it's safer to rely on your direction indicators, if fitted.

Arm signals at pedestrian crossings When slowing down or stopping at a pedestrian crossing consider using an arm signal. This tells

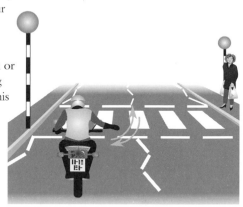

- Following traffic
- Approaching traffic
- Waiting pedestrians

that you're slowing down.

Remember, approaching traffic and pedestrians can't see your brake lights.

Arm signals aren't a substitute for faulty direction indicators. The law requires that if direction indicators are fitted they must work.

Direction indicator signals

Indicator lamps are close together on a motorcycle and can be difficult to see. On some smaller machines the direction indicators don't show up very well in bright sunlight.

- Consider giving an arm signal if you think your direction indicators are difficult to see
- Position yourself correctly and in good time for the manoeuvre you intend to perform

I intend to move in to the left or turn left or stop on the left

I intend to move out to the right or turn right

Timing of signals

Whether you're giving arm signals or using direction indicators

- Give your signal early enough to allow other road users to see and act on it
- Don't give a signal so early that its meaning could mislead

The illustration shows how a signal given too early could mislead. The driver of the red car might pull out, thinking the motorcyclist is turning.

Conflicting signals

A signal must have one clear meaning. For example, signalling right to pass a parked vehicle might mislead. Other traffic may think that you intend to turn right or to pull over on the right. Avoid giving signals which could have two meanings.

Cancelling signals Very few motorcycles have self-cancelling indicators. It's very important that you cancel a signal when you've completed the manoeuvre. Failure to cancel a signal could mislead another road user and cause an accident.

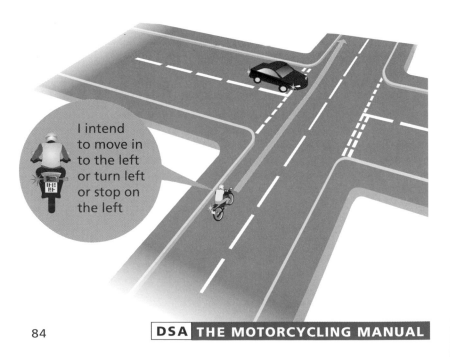

I intend to move in to the left or turn left or stop on the left

I am
slowing
down or
stopping

Other types of signals

Stop lamps   Stop lamps come on when you apply the brakes. On a modern motorcycle the stop lamps are activated by the rear brake pedal. On many machines the front brake lever will also activate the stop lamps.

The stop lamps warn following traffic that you're braking. Help other road users by

• Braking in good time

• Slowing down gradually

• Signalling in good time. Give an arm signal if necessary

Flashing headlamps   You should only flash your headlamp as an alternative to the horn to warn others that you're there. Assume that other drivers mean the same.

Don't flash at anyone to go ahead or turn.

If someone flashes their headlamps at you make sure that

• You understand what they mean

• It's you they're signalling to

Never assume it's a signal to proceed.

Horn   Sound the horn only if

• You think someone may not have seen you

• To warn other road users of your presence, for example at blind bends or junctions

Sounding the horn doesn't give you the right of way. Always be prepared to stop.

Never use your horn as a rebuke or to attract attention.

On high-speed roads drivers may not be able to hear your horn. In daylight, riding with your dipped headlamp on helps you to be seen.

Whether using indicators, arm signals, headlamps or horn, always think about your signal.

• Is it necessary?

• Is it helpful?

• Is it misleading?

When you do signal

• Signal in good time

• Signal clearly

• Signal correctly

Leave other road users in no doubt about your intentions. Giving signals properly is an important part of safe motorcycling.

Looking behind

When you ride on the road you need to be aware of the traffic behind you.

Before you change direction or speed you must know how your actions will affect following traffic. You also have to know when traffic is likely to overtake or come alongside you.

To check for traffic behind you can either

- Turn and look behind
- Look in your mirrors

Not all motorcycles are fitted with mirrors, and mirrors don't always give a clear view behind. There will be times when you need to look round to see the full picture. Looking behind also warns other drivers that you may be about to signal or alter course.

When should you look behind?

You may need to look behind well before you signal or make any manoeuvre or change of direction, for example before

- Moving off
- Turning left or right
- Overtaking
- Changing lanes
- Slowing or stopping

Normally look over your right shoulder and over your left shoulder before moving or turning to the left.

Warning   Looking over your shoulder too often or at the wrong moment can be hazardous. In the time you take to look behind you

- Lose touch with what's going on in front
- Run the risk of veering off course

At high speed or in congested moving traffic your attention needs to be focused ahead. In these situations time your rearward checks carefully. Combine

- Regular and sensible use of the mirrors
- The 'lifesaver' glance into the blind area before altering course

The 'lifesaver' glance

This is a final, quick rearward glance before you manoeuvre. This action makes you aware of what is happening behind and alongside before you alter course. This glance must be timed so that you still have time to react if it isn't safe to perform your manoeuvre.

Never forget to use it.

The blind area

The blind area is the area behind and to either side of you which isn't covered by mirrors. It's very important to check for traffic in this area before

- Moving off
- Changing direction
- Changing lane

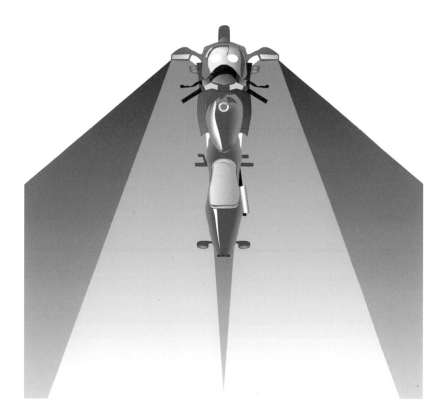

Mirrors

Mirrors must be adjusted to give a clear view behind. They should be kept clean and smear-free.

When you're riding you might find that your elbows or shoulders obstruct the view behind. To overcome this, adjust your mirrors to the best position. If this problem remains you can solve it by extending the mirrors with longer stems.

If your mirrors vibrate your view will be distorted. Your motorcycle dealer may be able to offer advice on how to reduce the vibration.

Using the mirrors

Glancing regularly into your mirrors will keep you up to date with the traffic situation behind. Use your mirrors before

- Signalling
- Changing direction
- Overtaking
- Changing lanes
- Slowing down or stopping

Use your mirrors together with rear observation, where necessary.

Just looking isn't enough!

Whether you look in your mirrors or over your shoulder

- You must act on what you see
- Think about how your actions will affect following traffic

Road position

As a general rule, keep to the centre of the lane. On a single carriageway (two-way traffic) that is halfway between the centre of the road and the left side.

Your position will depend on

- The width of the road
- The road surface
- Your view ahead
- Any obstructions

Your position should allow you to

- Be easily seen by traffic ahead, particularly vehicles emerging from junctions
- Be seen in the mirror of any vehicle in front
- Move over smoothly to the left to help overtaking traffic to come past safely

Keep clear of the gutter, where there are often pot-holes and loose grit.

Keep clear of the centre of the road. You might

- Obstruct overtaking traffic
- Put yourself in danger from oncoming traffic
- Encourage following traffic to overtake you on your left

Following large vehicles

When following large vehicles, such as lorries and buses, keep well back. This will

- Let you see past the vehicle in front
- Allow the driver in front to see you in his mirrors

Heavy and slow-moving traffic

It's often possible for motorcyclists to filter between lines of slow-moving or stationary traffic. Don't swerve or make unpredictable movements, and watch out for

- Vehicles suddenly changing lane or direction
- Vehicles emerging from junctions, which are hidden from view by the traffic
- Pedestrians

On bends

As you approach bends look out for

- Road signs warning you of a bend (see *The Highway Code*)
- The word 'SLOW' on the road
- Chevrons, indicating a sharp deviation

If you have to slow down do so before you reach the bend. Your machine is most stable if it's driven around a bend under light acceleration. Don't coast around a bend with the clutch lever pulled in.

Your view of the bend High hedges, fences and walls can reduce your view. Adjust your speed to suit the visibility, and be ready to stop.

Right-hand bends Keep to the left to improve your view. Watch out for

- Uneven surfaces
- Adverse camber

When taking a right-hand bend, don't ride too close to the centre line. Your head might cross over to the other side of the road as you bank over.

DSA THE MOTORCYCLING MANUAL

Left-hand bends On a left-hand bend keep to your normal road position. Don't move out into the centre of the road, where you may endanger yourself by getting too close to the oncoming traffic.

The road camber may work to your advantage, but don't go too fast.

Look out for

- Pedestrians, especially when there is no footpath
- Horse riders
- Stopped or broken-down vehicles
- Vehicles waiting to turn right

Always ride at such a speed that you can stop safely in the distance you can see to be clear.

Road junctions

A junction is where two or more roads meet. Look for indications of a junction ahead, such as

- Warning signs
- Road markings
- Direction signs
- Priority signs
- Give way and stop signs
- Traffic lights
- A break in the line of buildings
- A change in road surface

There are five main types of junction

- T-junctions
- Y-junctions
- Staggered junctions
- Crossroads
- Roundabouts

Many accidents occur at junctions as a result of poor observation or carelessness. Whichever type of junction you're dealing with, take care.

T-junctions

You'll find these where a minor road joins a major road from the left or right. The minor road will have either

- A stop sign and road markings
- A give way sign and road markings

- Give way lines only
- No road sign or markings

If you're riding on the major road

- Take note of any road signs and markings
- Watch for vehicles turning or emerging
- Avoid overtaking on the approach to a T-junction

If you're riding on the minor road

- Take note of the road signs
- Look for slippery surfaces or loose chippings
- Stop before emerging if your view into the major road is blocked in any way

Y-junctions

At a Y-junction the minor road joins the major road at an acute angle. Take care because a Y-junction can be deceptive. You may only have to make a slight change of direction to emerge.

Staggered junctions

These are junctions where roads join from both right and left. At a staggered junction the side roads don't join directly opposite one another but are slightly offset.

If you're riding on the major road look for

- Advance warning signs
- Vehicles emerging from either side
- Traffic turning into the side roads
- Vehicles crossing from one minor road into another

If you're emerging from either minor road

- Watch for traffic approaching in both directions
- Watch for traffic emerging from the road opposite
- Look for slippery surfaces

If you're crossing from one minor road into another take extra care. If there's room and it's safe, emerge to the centre of the major road. Wait for a safe opportunity to complete the manoeuvre. If there isn't enough room make sure that the gap in the traffic is wide enough in both directions. If in doubt, wait.

Crossroads

At a crossroads two side roads join a major road directly opposite each other. Crossroads are often accident black spots, so take extra care.

When going ahead on the major road look for vehicles emerging that might not have seen you. Where the roads are narrow and the view restricted slow down as you approach the junction.

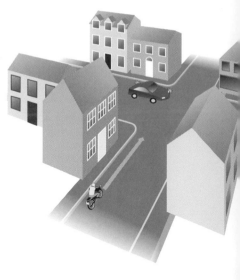

Unmarked crossroads Treat unmarked crossroads with extreme caution since neither road has priority.

Turning at crossroads The procedure for turning at crossroads is much the same as at any other junction.

Turning offside to offside gives you the chance to see approaching traffic. If you turn nearside to nearside your view of approaching traffic may be obscured. Turn offside to offside unless

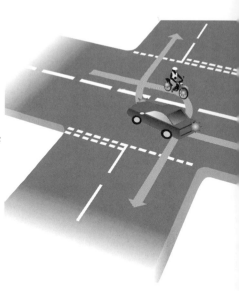

- Road markings dictate otherwise
- Other road users turn in front of you. If you're forced to turn nearside to nearside, wait until you can see it's safe to turn

Passing side roads

Look out for road signs indicating side roads, even if you aren't turning off. Often views are obscured at urban junctions. A driver may not see you and pull out in front of you.

If you doubt that a driver in a side road has seen you slow down and sound your horn. Be prepared to stop, if necessary.

Make yourself easy to see. Wear bright clothing and have your headlamp on dipped beam **at all times.**

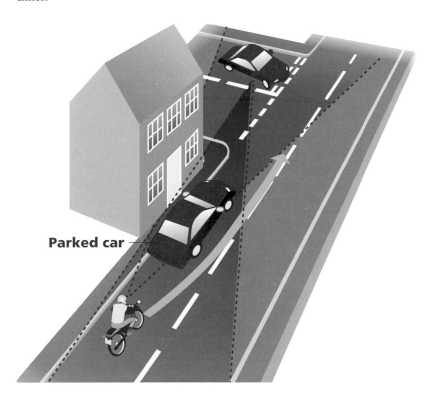

Parked car

Roundabouts

Roundabouts allow traffic from different roads to merge without necessarily stopping.

Before you enter a roundabout

- Use road signs to help you plan your route
- Give way to traffic on your immediate right

Keep moving if the way is clear.

Going left

- Indicate left as you approach and ride through the roundabout
- Approach in the left-hand lane
- Keep to the left lane through the roundabout
- Cancel the left signal when you've completed the turn

Going ahead

- Approach in the left lane (unless road markings direct you otherwise). If you can't use the left lane because it's blocked use the next available lane
- Don't give any signal as you approach the roundabout
- Keep to the left lane around the roundabout (unless road markings direct you otherwise)
- Indicate left as you pass the exit before the one you intend to take
- You may need to take a 'lifesaver' glance to check that it's safe to leave the roundabout
- Make sure that you cancel the signal when you've completed the manoeuvre

Going right

- Indicate right as you approach and maintain that signal on the roundabout

- Approach in the right-hand lane. Keep to the right-hand lane on the roundabout. Be aware that traffic may be passing on your left

- Indicate left as you pass the exit before the one you intend to take

- Take a 'lifesaver' glance over your left shoulder to check that it's safe to leave the roundabout

- Cancel the signal when you've completed the turn

Changed priority Occasionally traffic on a roundabout has to give way to traffic entering. Watch out for give way signs and lines as you ride around a roundabout.

Mini-roundabouts These have the same rules as other roundabouts. At a mini-roundabout

- There's less space and time to signal and manoeuvre

- Traffic travels very quickly across the junction, due to the small size. Make sure that you have enough time to enter safely

- Beware of drivers who are using the roundabout for a U-turn

- Beware of drivers who don't signal correctly

- Avoid riding on the painted area, especially in the wet

Road surface The road surface at a roundabout can become polished and slippery especially when wet. Fuel oil spillage on roundabouts can also make the road very slippery.

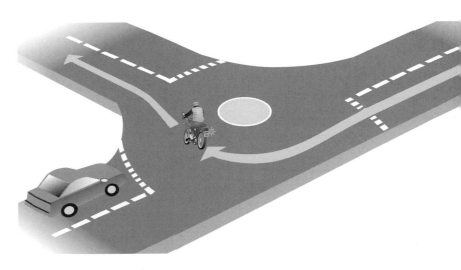

Emerging

When a rider leaves one road and joins or crosses another this is called 'emerging'.

At a junction you'll have to decide whether it's

- Necessary to wait
- Safe to emerge

Your decision to emerge depends largely on how much you can see. If you can't see clearly you must

- Stop at the edge of the road you're joining
- Ease forward until you're in a position where you can see clearly. Take care not to edge out into the path of passing traffic

You must stop if the road signs direct you to.

Being able to judge the speed and distance of other traffic is a skill. Don't emerge if you'll impede the progress of other road users. At busy junctions you may have to be patient and wait for a safe opportunity to emerge. Don't be tempted to

- Emerge when you shouldn't
- Force your way into a stream of traffic

After you emerge

- Make sure that you cancel your signal
- Check behind for the speed and position of other traffic
- Accelerate so that your speed is correct for the road and conditions
- Keep a safe distance from the vehicle in front

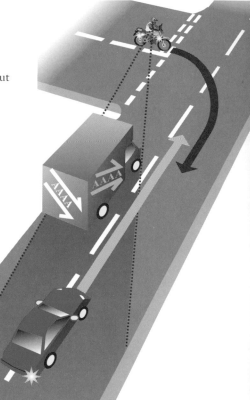

Defensive riding is based on good observation and anticipation.

On today's roads it's important that you look and plan well ahead. Avoid putting yourself in a situation where you're trying to do too many things at once.

Question the intentions of other road users and try to anticipate their actions. Anticipation is a skill which develops with experience. This part describes the main features of defensive riding which will help you to safely gain that experience. Use these techniques whenever you ride.

The topics covered

- Observation
- Hazards
- Junctions
- Overtaking
- Separation distance
- Dual carriageways
- Lighting conditions
- Other road users

Observation

Zone of vision

The area you can see from your riding position is known as your 'zone of vision'. When you're riding your zone of vision is constantly changing. You need to be alert and on the lookout for possible hazards. Your zone of vision will influence how fast you ride. If you can't see clearly ahead, slow down and be prepared to stop.

At junctions How you deal with a junction will depend on your zone of vision. As you get closer to a junction your zone of vision usually improves. Make sure that you can see clearly into a junction before deciding to emerge.

At some junctions your view may be severely restricted and so you'll have to stop.

• Edge forward to a position from which you have a clear view before deciding to emerge

• Look in every direction

• Keep looking as you emerge

• Don't commit yourself until you've seen it's safe to continue

You can use the term LAD to help you deal with junctions. LAD stands for

• Look

• Assess

• Decide (wait or go)

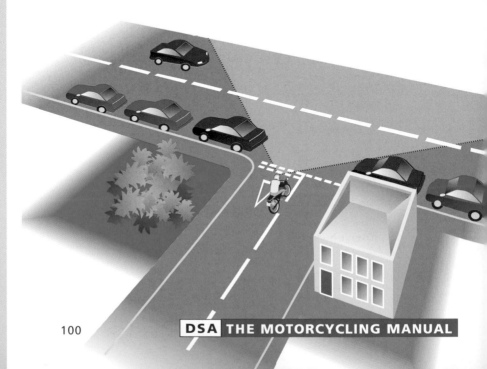

Being seen

As you approach a junction where you can see a vehicle waiting to emerge, ask yourself

- Can the driver see me?
- Am I sure I've been seen?
- Have I an escape route if I haven't been seen?

Many collision accidents happen at road junctions when a driver doesn't see a motorcyclist.

Daytime use of dipped headlamps and wearing bright clothing increase your chances of being seen. Improving your visibility is an important aspect of defensive riding.

Hazards

A hazard is any situation which involves you in some risk or danger.

The action you need to take will vary from one hazard to another. Any action which demands a change of speed or course is called a manoeuvre. A manoeuvre can vary from slowing slightly to turning on a very busy road.

The OSM routine

The OSM routine will enable you to cope safely with hazards. OSM stands for

- Observation
- Signal
- Manoeuvre

Observation Check the position of following traffic using your mirrors or by taking direct rear observation at an appropriate time.

Signal If necessary, signal your intention to change course or speed. Signal clearly and in good time.

Manoeuvre Carry out the manoeuvre, if it's safe to do so. Manoeuvring has three phases

- Position
- Speed
- Look

Consider each phase in turn and use them all as appropriate to the situation.

The PSL routine

Position Get into the correct position in good time to negotiate the hazard. This helps other road users to see what you intend to do. Positioning yourself too late can be dangerous.

Speed Slow down as you approach a hazard. Make sure that you don't leave it too late. Always be ready to stop.

Look Keep looking to assess all possible dangers. You need to know the traffic situation behind as well as in front.

If you're joining a road, keep looking as you turn from one road to the other.

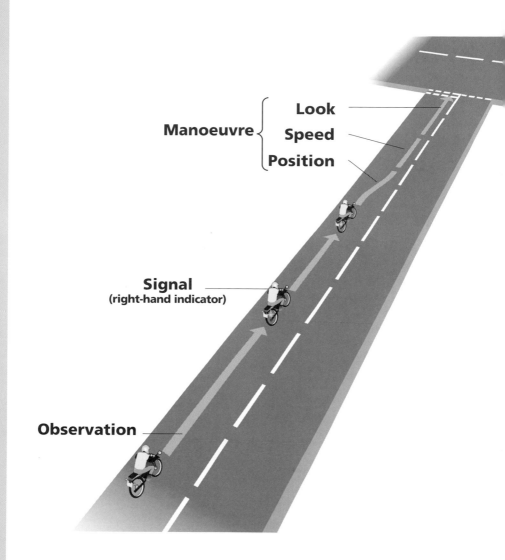

Manoeuvre
Look
Speed
Position

Signal
(right-hand indicator)

Observation

Spotting hazards

It's important that you're able to recognise and react to hazards before they develop into emergencies.

In the illustration the rider must pull out to pass the parked lorry, but

- Is the blue car really going to turn left? The driver may have forgotten to cancel the indicator from a previous turn

- If the blue car does turn, will the pedestrian decide to cross? Has the rider seen or anticipated the pedestrian?

- Which way is the red car going to turn?

If you're travelling too fast you won't be able to cope with everything at once. This illustrates the need for early recognition of hazards and appropriate speed adjustment.

Positioning   Ask yourself

- Can I see and be seen? When you're following a van or large goods vehicle, don't get too close behind. You won't be able to see the road ahead and the driver might not be able to see you in his mirrors

- Are other vehicles restricting my options?

- Have I enough room to get out of trouble? Allow plenty of room when passing parked cars

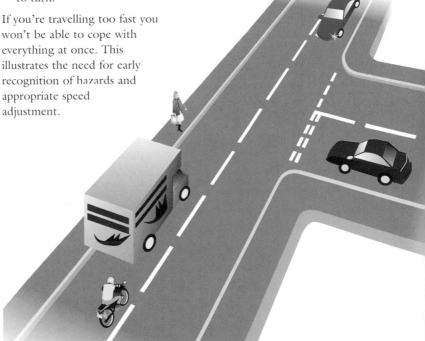

Allowing time and space Always leave yourself enough time and space to cope with what's ahead. The earlier you see the situation, the more time you have to anticipate and plan your actions. To get early information you need to

- Constantly change your field of view. Look far ahead and near, especially in towns where things change quickly
- Regularly check on the situation behind
- Watch for clues about what's going to happen next

For example, a parked car could spell danger if

- The driver or a passenger is sitting in it
- The engine is running. Vapour coming from the exhaust is an obvious clue

Be prepared in case

- A door is thrown open suddenly
- The car moves off without warning

Keep a lookout for pedestrians who may walk out between parked vehicles. Children are especially difficult to see because of their small size.

Speed Ask yourself

- Could I stop in time if the vehicle in front braked sharply?
- Am I going too fast? You must take the road and traffic conditions into account at all times
- Am I going too slowly? Exaggerated caution can create hazards and impede the normal traffic flow

Your safety This lies largely in your own hands. The better your management of your machine and roadspace, the safer you should be.

Junctions

Approaching junctions

At every junction use the OSM/PSL routine.

Observation   Look all around so that you're aware of the traffic situation.

Signal   You should signal clearly and in good time.

Manoeuvre   Use the PSL routine.

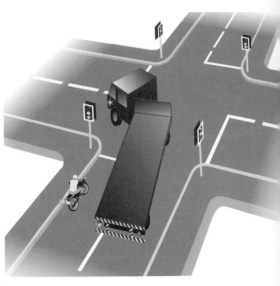

Position   If the road has no lane markings

- When turning left, keep to the left
- When turning right, keep as close to the centre of the road as is safe. In a one-way street move to the right-hand side of the road in good time

If the road has lane markings

- Use the correct lane for the direction you intend to take
- Move into the lane as soon as you can

Speed   Adjust your speed as necessary.

Look   Watch for other traffic when you reach a point from which you can see.

In traffic don't

- Lose your patience
- Switch lanes to gain advantage over others

When you're moving ahead

- Make sure that you're in the correct lane
- Look out for vehicles changing lane, either with or without signalling

Articulated or long vehicles   Such vehicles may take up a position that seems wrong to you. At junctions and roundabouts don't be tempted to squeeze past. The rear wheels might cut across your path as the vehicle turns.

Turning at junctions

Turning left into a major road

Assess the junction. Check the road signs and markings. Use the OSM/PSL routine.

O – Look in your mirrors and take rear observation as necessary.

S – Signal left at the correct time.

M – Manoeuvre; use PSL.

P – Keep to the left.

S – Reduce speed. Be prepared to stop. Traffic on a minor road must give way to traffic on a major road.

L – Look in all directions at the earliest point from which you can see. Keep looking as you slow down, and stop if necessary.

You must be aware of pedestrians, cyclists and other motorcyclists who may be alongside. You also need to know how traffic behind is reacting to your manoeuvre.

Turning right into a major road

Assess the junction. Check road signs and markings. Use the OSM/PSL routine.

O – Look in your mirrors and take rear observation as necessary.

S – Signal right in good time.

M – Manoeuvre; use PSL.

P – Position yourself as close to the centre of the road as is safe.

In a one-way street, position yourself on the right-hand side of the road.

When turning right it's important to take up your position early.

S – Reduce speed. Be prepared to stop. You must give way to traffic on a major road.

L – Look in all directions at the earliest point from which you can see. Keep looking as you slow down, and stop if necessary.

Take a 'lifesaver' glance over your right shoulder before you turn. Take this glance early enough for you to change your plan if it isn't safe to turn.

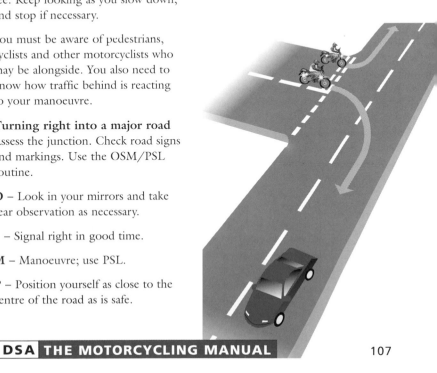

Turning right into a side road
Assess the junction and use the OSM/PSL routine. Check the road signs and markings.

O – Look in your mirrors and take rear observation as necessary.

S – Signal right in good time.

M – Manoeuvre; use PSL.

P – Position yourself as close to the centre of the road as is safe, so that vehicles can pass on your left.

In a one-way street, keep to the right-hand side of the road.

S – Adjust your speed as necessary. Watch out for aproaching traffic. Stop if necessary.

L – Look into the road you're joining. Watch for vehicles waiting to emerge and pedestrians crossing the road.

Take a 'lifesaver' glance over your right shoulder just before you turn. Do this early enough for you to change your plan if it isn't safe to turn.

Avoid cutting the corner. (Enter on the left-hand side of the road.)

When you've completed the turn

- Cancel your signal
- Check for following traffic
- Accelerate progressively up to the speed suitable for the road and traffic conditions within the set speed limit

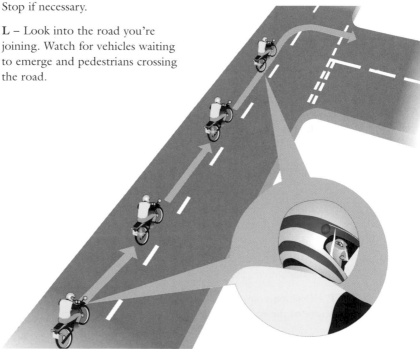

DSA THE MOTORCYCLING MANUAL

Turning left into a side road

Assess the junction and use the OSM/PSL routine. Check the road signs and markings.

O – Look in your mirrors and take rear observation as necessary.

S – Signal left at the correct time.

M – Manoeuvre; use PSL.

P – Your position on approach shouldn't change significantly from your normal riding position. Don't swing out before or after the turn.

S – Left turns are often sharper than right turns, so reduce speed accordingly.

L – Look out for vehicles stopping just before the junction and pedestrians who may not have seen you. Don't overtake a cyclist just before the turn and then cut in just ahead. If you're riding slowly, watch for cyclists coming up on your left. A 'lifesaver' glance over your left shoulder before you turn may be necessary.

Take special care when

- Crossing a bicycle or bus lane
- Pedestrians are crossing or waiting to cross, especially children
- On a loose or slippery road surface

When you've completed the turn

- Cancel your signal
- Check behind so that you know what's following
- Assume the correct road position
- Accelerate progressively up to the speed suitable for the road and traffic conditions within the set speed limit

Overtaking

When you want to overtake use the OSM/PSL routine. Never overtake unless you're certain that it's safe to do so.

Don't overtake

- Unless it's necessary
- If your view ahead is blocked
- If other drivers might not be able to see you
- If there isn't enough room
- If the road narrows
- If you're approaching a junction
- If you're within the zigzag area of a pedestrian crossing
- If there's a no overtaking sign
- If you have to cross a continuous central white line on your side of the road. The exception to this rule is when it's safe to pass an obstruction such as a road maintenance vehicle, a cyclist or a horse. They must be either stationary or travelling at less than 10 mph
- If there's 'dead ground', that is, a dip in the road which might conceal an oncoming vehicle

General Procedure

To overtake, use the OSM/PSL routine.

O – Take observation, both well ahead and behind.

S – Consider signalling.

M – Manoeuvre; use PSL.

P – Check your position. Can you see ahead?

S – Have you enough speed and acceleration to overtake?

L – Look! Is it clear to overtake? How far away and how fast is traffic approaching?

If you have any doubts, don't overtake.

If you're satisfied that it's safe to continue with the overtake, apply OSM again.

When you overtake you should

- Take a 'lifesaver' glance just before you move out
- Overtake as quickly as you can and don't cut in front of the vehicle you've just passed
- Cancel your signal when you've finished overtaking
- Never automatically follow an overtaking vehicle. Your view of the road ahead may be obstructed. If you can't see clearly ahead, wait

Overtaking on the left

You may overtake on the left when

- The vehicle in front is turning right and there's enough room for you to pass safely on the left
- You want to turn left at a junction
- Traffic is moving slowly in queues and vehicles in the lane on your right are moving more slowly than you are
- Riding in a one-way street where vehicles are allowed to pass on either side (not to be confused with a dual carriageway)

Judging speed and distance

If you're travelling at 50 mph and an oncoming vehicle is travelling at the same speed, you're approaching each other at 100 mph or 45 metres (about 150 feet) per second. This can be difficult to judge accurately so give yourself plenty of time.

Take great care if you're travelling on a two-way three-lane road. An oncoming vehicle might pull out to overtake while you're overtaking. Wearing bright clothing and riding with your dipped headlamp on will help oncoming drivers to see you. Nevertheless, be aware of the possibility of a head-on collision.

When you're following slower traffic and looking for the chance to overtake, keep a safe distance. Staying back will help you to see past the vehicle in front, and give you time to react to its signals.

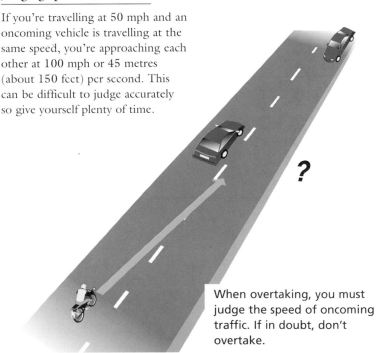

When overtaking, you must judge the speed of oncoming traffic. If in doubt, don't overtake.

Separation distance

How far must you keep from the vehicle in front? Ideally you should be no closer than the stopping distance that corresponds to your speed. In some traffic situations that may not be possible. The gap must never be less than your thinking distance, and much more if the road is wet or slippery.

One method of judging separation distance is to allow 1 metre (just over 3 feet) for each mph of your speed. For example, at 45 mph leave a gap of 45 metres (about 150 feet).

A useful technique for judging 1 metre per mph is to use the 'two-second rule'.

The two-second rule

In good conditions an experienced rider needs to be at least two seconds behind the vehicle in front.

To measure this gap

- Select a stationary object on the side of the road, for example a road sign

- As the vehicle in front passes the object say to yourself, 'Only a fool breaks the two-second rule.'

If you reach the object before you finish saying the sentence, you're too close.

In bad weather, at least double this gap between you and the vehicle in front.

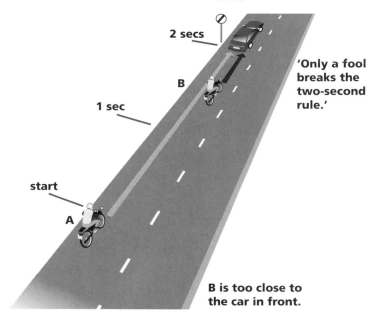

2 secs

B

1 sec

'Only a fool breaks the two-second rule.'

start

A

B is too close to the car in front.

Separation distance behind

When the vehicle behind is following too closely, slow down gradually. You need to increase the gap between you and the vehicle in front. This will

- Give you more time to brake if necessary
- Give the following vehicle a better chance to overtake

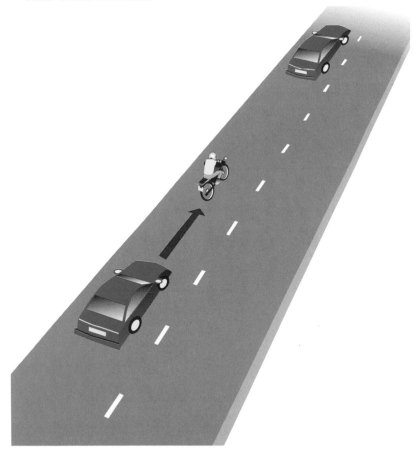

Dual carriageways

- Have at least two lanes in each direction
- Have a central reserve dividing streams of traffic. There may also be a safety barrier on the central reserve

Although some dual carriageways appear similar to motorways, the same regulations don't apply.

Beware of slow-moving vehicles such as farm tractors, cyclists and pedestrians.

Turning left onto a dual carriageway

If there's no acceleration lane or slip road

- Emerge as you would to turn left on a single carriageway
- Traffic may be travelling faster than on a single carriageway

If there's an acceleration lane or slip road

- Emerge as you would to join a motorway
- Use the acceleration lane to accelerate. Match your speed with that of traffic in the left-hand lane
- Move into a safe gap in the traffic

Remember to use a 'lifesaver' glance just before you move into the left lane.

Turning left from a dual carriageway

If there's no deceleration lane or slip road

- Signal your intentions clearly and in good time
- Slow down in good time

If there's a deceleration lane or slip road

- Signal in good time
- Don't reduce speed until you've moved into the deceleration lane
- Check your speedometer. If you've been riding at high speeds you may find yourself travelling faster than you realise

Turning right onto a dual carriageway

You'll have to cross the first carriageway before you can join the carriageway you want.

If the central reserve is wide enough

- You can wait in it for a gap in the traffic on the carriageway you want
- Don't leave yourself jutting out either side of the central reserve

If the central reserve is too narrow

- Wait until the dual carriageway is clear in both directions
- Traffic may be travelling at high speeds. If in doubt, wait for a large gap in the traffic

Turning right from a dual carriageway

The central reserve sometimes has gaps for turning right. These may have special filter lanes.

To turn right, use your mirrors and signal in good time. Don't forget a 'lifesaver' glance before you turn.

You may have to cross the path of fast oncoming vehicles in two or more lanes. If in doubt, wait.

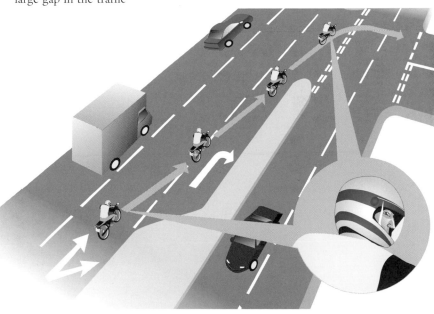

Overtaking on dual carriageways

Don't overtake unless you're sure that you can do so safely. Use the appropriate parts of the OSM/PSL routine.

O – Use your mirrors. Take rear observation if necessary.

P – Position yourself so that you can see well ahead past the vehicle in front.

S – Make sure that you have enough reserve speed to overtake.

L – Look ahead to make sure that the lane you want to join is clear.

If you're satisfied that it's safe to overtake, use OSM again.

M – Manoeuvre. Don't forget the 'lifesaver' glance into the blind area before you change course. Overtake quickly and decisively. Cancel your signal promptly and return to the left lane only when you're clear of the vehicle you've overtaken. Don't cut in.

High-speed riding   If you're travelling at high speed it's safer to combine regular, sensible use of the mirrors with the 'lifesaver' glance before changing course.

Lane discipline   Use the left-hand lane unless the amount of slow-moving traffic would cause you to be constantly changing lanes. Don't weave from lane to lane.

Where there are three lanes, don't ride in the middle lane if the left lane is clear. Always return to the left lane when you've finished overtaking.

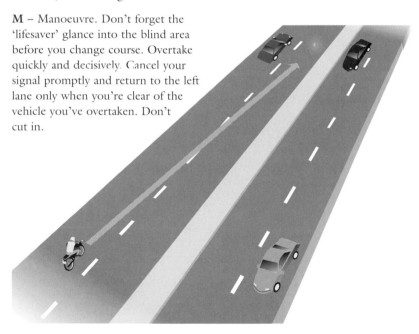

Lighting conditions

In the dark, seeing hazards is more difficult. The clues are there, but you have to pick them out. Look for

- Illuminated signs
- Reflective signs
- Reflectors between white lines
- The glow of vehicle headlights on buildings, trees and hedges indicating bends and junctions

In the dark

- It can be difficult to judge distances and speed from headlights
- Headlights on vehicles make it difficult to see pedestrians, cyclists and any vehicle with dim lights
- Don't let shop and advertising lights distract you
- Watch for zebra crossings, traffic lights and road signs

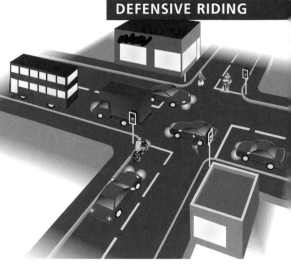

Wet roads

Wet roads increase reflected and distracting light. The reflections from wet surfaces make it more difficult to see unlit objects.

The combination of rain and darkness reduce visibility further. On unlit or poorly lit roads keep your speed down. Remember, your stopping distance will be increased while your visibility is reduced.

Unlit side view

When you're sideways on to other road users you'll be less easily seen, for example when

- Passing side turnings
- Emerging right or left

Wearing reflective material will help passing drivers to see you.

Other road users

Cyclists

Make allowances for cyclists, especially children. The younger the cyclist, the more you must watch them. Cyclists might

- Glance round, showing they might move out or turn

- Make sudden sideways movements into your path

- Be carrying objects that could affect their control and balance

- Weave about, slow down or stop to push their bike up a hill

- Emerge without looking where cycle routes rejoin the carriageway

Pedestrians

When turning from one road to another

- Give way to pedestrians who are crossing

- Look for pedestrians who may step off the pavement without looking. If you don't think they've seen you, sound your horn

At pedestrian crossings, never overtake within the zigzag area of a zebra or pelican crossing.

Children Take extra care where children may be about, particularly near schools at the start and finish of the school day.

Children sometimes play in the road. If you see any signs, such as a ball bouncing across the road, reduce your speed.

Disabled pedestrians Take special care with the visually handicapped or disabled – they may not be able to judge speed and distance accurately. If a pedestrian is hard of hearing or deaf it won't be immediately obvious. Take extra care if a pedestrian fails to look your way as you approach.

Animals

Animals are easily frightened by

- Noise

- Vehicles coming too close to them

Give animals as much room as possible and don't

- Sound the horn

- Rev the engine

Be particularly careful when approaching horses, especially when ridden by children.

If someone in charge of animals signals to you to stop, do so and switch off your engine.

Motorways are designed to help traffic move quickly and safely over long distances. They place demands on both the rider and machine that are different to those of other roads. For example, the effect of weather conditions can be exaggerated by higher speeds.

High-speed riding means that situations can develop rapidly so you need to be alert and feeling well. Use the two-second rule and look well ahead. Don't just focus on the vehicle in front.

On a motorway you'll find that you're exposed to wind turbulence, particularly from larger vehicles. Anticipate the wind effect and make sure that you keep full control of your machine.

The topics covered

- Motorway riding
- Joining the motorway
- Motorway road signs
- Lane discipline
- Overtaking
- Motorway weather conditions
- Breakdowns
- Leaving the motorway

Motorway riding

Before you can ride on a motorway you must hold a full motorcycle licence. (Learner riders aren't allowed on motorways.)

Birmingham
M1
25
1m

Mopeds and motorcycles under 50cc aren't allowed to use the motorway.

Due to the demanding nature of motorways make sure that

- You have a thorough knowledge of the sections of the *The Highway Code* dealing with motorways
- You know and understand the motorway warning signs and signals

Make sure that your motorcycle is well prepared for motorway travel. Check that

- You have enough fuel to enable you to reach your destination or a motorway service area
- Your tyres are correctly inflated and show no obvious defects
- Your lights and indicators are working properly
- Any load is securely fastened

Long motorway journeys can be tiring so plan your route and use the service areas. Don't attempt a long journey if you feel tired or unwell.

On motorways, make sure that other drivers can see you. Wear high-visibility clothing and ride with your headlamp on dipped beam.

Joining the motorway

You'll normally join the motorway from a slip road on the left. This then leads into an acceleration lane.

Use the acceleration lane to increase your speed up to that of traffic already on the motorway. Look for a gap in the traffic and move out into the left-hand lane when it's safe. Don't forget a 'lifesaver' glance before you move across.

Stay in the left-hand lane long enough to acclimatise to the speed and traffic flow.

Other vehicles joining

After passing an exit there's usually an entry where other vehicles join. Don't try to compete with them. Move across to the next lane if it's safe, or reduce speed and let them join ahead of you.

Motorway road signs

Motorway signs can be found

- On the left-hand side of the road
- On the central reserve
- On overhead gantries

The signs are positioned to help you to see them from a distance. This should help you to plan ahead.

Look out for flashing amber lights – these warn of danger ahead. Look for the signs which could indicate

- Lane closures
- Speed limits
- Roadworks
- Other hazards

Some signals have red lights. If the red lights flash above your lane, you must not go beyond the signal in that lane. If the red lights flash on a slip road, you must not enter the motorway at this point.

Lane discipline

Change lane only if necessary. When you do change lane, use the OSM routine in good time. At higher speeds you need to give other drivers more time to react. Always remember your 'lifesaver' check.

Two-lane motorways

Use the left-hand lane for normal riding. Use the right-hand lane for overtaking only. Return to the left-hand lane after overtaking.

Three or more lanes

Use the left-hand lane for normal riding. The right-hand lanes are for overtaking only. When the left-hand lane has a lot of slow-moving traffic stay in the second or third lane while you're overtaking. Avoid repeatedly moving in and then pulling out again almost immediately. Return to the left lane after overtaking.

The right-hand lane isn't a 'fast lane'. It's for overtaking only.

Overtaking

Before you overtake, plan well ahead and use those parts of the OSM/PSL routine that apply.

O – Use the mirrors to assess the speed, course and position of following traffic.

P – Position yourself so that you can see well past the vehicle in front.

S – Make sure that your machine has the speed capability to overtake without struggling.

L – Look to ensure that the lane you want to join is clear.

O – Use the mirrors again to check the situation behind. Traffic might be coming up faster than you think.

S – Signal early to give other drivers time to react.

M – Don't forget the 'lifesaver' glance before altering course. When it's safe, pull out into the overtaking lane and then cancel your signal.

As you overtake a large goods vehicle, bus or coach you'll be buffeted by the changing air pressure. Don't ride too close to the vehicle you're overtaking.

In queues of slow-moving traffic you may overtake on the left if the traffic in the right lane is moving slower than that in the left lane.

Don't swap lanes to gain advantage and don't use the hard shoulder for overtaking.

Motorway weather conditions

When you ride on motorways the most common weather problems will be

- Crosswinds
- Rain
- Fog

Crosswinds

You need to be especially careful

- As you come out from the shelter of a large vehicle when overtaking or being overtaken
- On exposed stretches

Keep your speed down where there is a danger of crosswinds. Riding more slowly will help you to keep control.

Rain

In heavy rain the surface spray from other vehicles will seriously reduce visibility, as well as increase stopping distance. Make sure that

- You're visible. Use dipped headlights and wear bright clothing

- You can see clearly. Keep your visor or goggles clean

Fog

In fog you need to

- Slow down and keep your distance from the vehicle ahead
- Use dipped headlamps and rear fog lamps (if fitted) when visibility falls below 100 metres (about 330 feet)
- Make sure that your visor or goggles are clean and aren't hindering your view ahead
- Wear bright clothing. This will help other drivers to see you

CROSSWIND

CROSSWIND

Drop in pressur[e] can pull rider towards large vehicle

Coloured reflective studs

These are used on all motorways and some other roads. They help you to find your position on the road in poor visibility.

The colours are

- **Red:** along the left-hand edge of the carriageway
- **Amber:** along the right-hand edge of the carriageway
- **Green:** along the left-hand edge, where slip roads leave or join the motorway
- **White:** between lanes

Breakdowns

If your machine breaks down, try to get onto the hard shoulder.

Never attempt even minor repairs on the hard shoulder. Make your way to the nearest emergency telephone and call for assistance. Marker posts will direct you to the nearest telephone.

To rejoin the motorway

Don't pull straight out onto the carriageway. Use the hard shoulder as an acceleration lane to build up speed before joining the left-hand lane when there's a gap.

Stopping on motorways

You must not stop on motorways unless

- It's an emergency
- You want to prevent an accident
- Police or road signs indicate that you must

If you need to stop for a rest, find a service area. The hard shoulder is for emergencies only. It isn't for parking or resting.

Obstructions

If vehicles ahead switch on their hazard warning lights be prepared for slow-moving or stopped traffic.

Look well ahead and leave yourself plenty of room. Check behind to see how the following traffic is reacting.

If you find yourself catching up with slower-moving traffic there could be an obstruction ahead. Be aware that other vehicles may be slowing gradually without the need to brake. You won't have warning from their brake lights in these situations.

Leaving the motorway

You'll see

- Signs one mile and half a mile before each exit
- Countdown markers at 300, 200 and 100 yards from the slip road

Move to the left-hand lane well before you reach the slip road. Signal in good time but maintain your speed until you've moved onto the slip road (traffic conditions permitting).

As you ride along the slip road, check your speedometer. You may be travelling faster than you think.

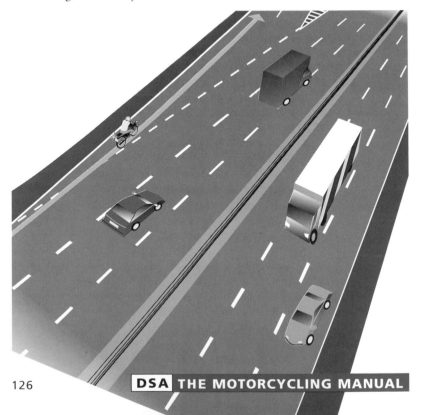

The weather in the British Isles is varied and uncertain. You can expect to encounter virtually all weather conditions at some time.

The weather presents particular hazards for the motorcyclist. You need to think about how you're going to

- Protect yourself from the elements
- Adapt your riding to suit the conditions

As you gain experience you'll find that it pays to be prepared for the worst kind of weather for the time of year. You'll also find that there are some weather conditions when it's better not to ride at all.

The topics covered

- **Rain**
- **Mist and fog**
- **Cold weather**
- **Wind**
- **Hot weather**

Rain

Rain presents three main problems to you when you ride a motorcycle

- Keeping dry
- Seeing and being seen
- Dealing with a wet road

Keeping dry

If you allow yourself to get wet you'll also get cold. Being cold and wet can seriously reduce your ability to concentrate.

Proper motorcycle clothing is available which will keep you dry in the heaviest downpour. Good motorcycle clothing is a must if you intend to ride in bad weather.

Seeing and being seen

Heavy rain on your visor or goggles can affect your view of the road. If you can't see clearly, slow down and stop. If your visor or goggles have fogged up on the inside, wipe them clean.

Some modern helmets have air vents to help prevent visors from fogging up. Anti-fog sprays are also available.

Making yourself visible to other road users is important at all times. In the rain it's especially so, due to the reduction in visibility caused by the rain.

Dealing with a wet road

A wet road means

- Less efficient braking
- A longer distance to stop
- A greater risk of skidding

If the surface is good but wet

- Aim to brake when the machine is in its most stable position, that is, upright and moving straight ahead
- Apply the front brake slightly before the rear. Spread the braking effort evenly between the front and rear brakes

Wet metal drain covers are a special hazard for motorcyclists. Try to avoid them if you can do so safely.

layer of
water

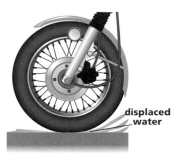

displaced
water

Surface water

When the rain is very heavy or if the road has poor drainage you'll have to deal with surface water. If you ride too fast through surface water your tyres might not be able to displace water quickly enough. A film of water will build up between the tyre and the road and skidding can occur. The effect is called 'aquaplaning'. Worn tyres will increase the risk of aquaplaning.

Try not to splash pedestrians by riding through pools of water close to the kerb.

Floods

If you have to ride through a flood

• Ride slowly in a low gear and keep your engine running fast enough to keep water out of the exhaust

• Try to ride where the water is most shallow. Watch for oncoming vehicles who may be doing the same thing

• Test your brakes when you're out of the water

Mist and fog

Mist and fog can be very deceptive. One of the dangers of fog is its patchy nature.

If you find yourself in fog

- Slow down so that you can stop within your range of vision
- Use your dipped headlight
- Keep your visor or goggles clear
- Keep your distance from the vehicle in front
- Use your rear fog lamp (if fitted) when visibility falls below 100 metres (about 330 feet)

Riding in very dense fog can be disorientating and frightening. This is one occasion when you need to ask yourself, is your journey really necessary?

Positioning

Don't ride near the centre of the road. Oncoming traffic might pass dangerously close. Don't ride in the gutter either as parked vehicles, cyclists and pedestrians could appear suddenly.

Junctions

Be specially careful at junctions and where you aren't able to see other traffic. In fog, traffic will generally be moving more slowly and you might not be able to hear it approaching.

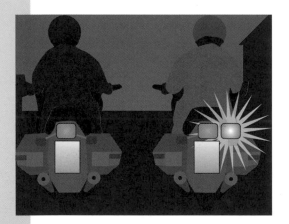

DSA THE MOTORCYCLING MANUAL

Cold weather

If you get cold when motorcycling

- Your concentration will suffer
- Your ability to control your machine will be affected
- Your enjoyment of motorcycling will be lessened

Keeping warm can be a problem. There is motorcycle clothing available which will keep you warm in very low temperatures. This clothing isn't cheap, but it's essential if you want to ride in cold weather.

The cold will probably affect your hands and feet first. Don't continue if you lose feeling in your fingers or toes. Stop now and then to warm up.

Black ice

Black ice is very dangerous. It forms when droplets of water freeze on a normally good skid-resistant surface. Black ice is so dangerous because it's almost invisible.

In wintry conditions, if the road looks wet but you can't hear tyre noise as you would on a wet road, suspect black ice.

Snow

It's better not to ride at all in conditions of ice and snow. If you must ride in snow and ice keep to the main roads. These are more likely to be clear and well gritted. In falling snow, use your dipped headlight and keep your visor or goggles clear. Snow will quickly cover road signs and markings. Be aware of the danger this creates.

Wind

Strong crosswinds can suddenly blow you off course

- As you pass gateways or gaps in hedges
- As you pass gaps in buildings
- As you pass high-sided vehicles
- On exposed roads

When it's windy keep your speed down so that you can remain in control. Look ahead and anticipate places where crosswinds may affect you.

Crosswinds can affect other road users too. Take care when overtaking

- Cyclists
- High-sided vehicles
- Vehicles towing trailers or caravans

Hot weather

Motorcycling is probably at its best during warm, dry weather.

When the weather becomes very hot the road surface can start to melt. Melted tar can reduce tyre grip and lead to skidding.

During a long hot, dry spell the road surface will become coated with rubber, particularly at

- Junctions
- Bends
- Roundabouts

When it rains after such a dry spell the road will be unusually slippery. Look out for shiny surfaces.

Never ride
- **In shorts or trainers**
- **Bare-armed**

Always wear full protective clothing.

DSA THE MOTORCYCLING MANUAL

Riding at night is another aspect of motorcycling which demands special techniques and precautions. The problems of riding at night vary with the type of road and the amount of traffic, but this part deals with the most important aspects.

The topics covered

- Seeing
- Lights
- Being seen

If you're riding in poor visibility or in the dark don't wear

- Sunglasses
- Tinted goggles
- A tinted visor

Seeing

The two main requirements for riding at night are seeing and being seen.

To help you see at night

- Keep your goggles or visor clean. Scratches on either can cause dazzle from approaching traffic. If your goggles or visor become scratched you should replace them
- Make sure that your headlamp is clean and correctly adjusted
- Practise operating the light switches so that you can find them quickly in the dark

If you doubt your ability to see in the dark, have your eyesight checked.

Lights

Using dipped beam

You must use dipped headlights

- At night when street lighting is poor (street lights more than 185 metres (600 feet) apart)
- In poor visibility
- At night on all other roads including motorways

To help other road users to see you, ride with dipped headlights on at all times – even in good daylight.

Dazzle If you're dazzled by oncoming lights

- Slow down and stop if necessary
- Keep your headlight on dipped beam

Don't flash your main beam.

Using main beam

Use your headlight on main beam in any conditions where the main beam will help you to see without dazzling other road users.

When your headlight is on main beam the blue 'main beam warning lamp' will glow.

Dipping your headlights Dip your main beam

- In the face of oncoming traffic
- When approaching traffic from behind

Don't dazzle other road users – you could cause an accident.

When you dip your headlights

- You'll see less of the road ahead
- Slow down so that you can stop within the distance you can see

Being seen

At night it's more difficult for other road users to see you in good time. In congested urban areas a single motorcycle headlight can get lost in the background of distracting lights.

Be aware of the difficulty other road users might have and

- Ride with dipped headlights, unless you need to use the full beam
- Wear reflective clothing. Fluorescent clothing won't show in the dark
- Keep your lamps clean and working correctly. Carry a spare set of bulbs and fuses
- Keep your (reflective) number plate clean

Riding with a passenger or a load can call for adjustments to your machine as well as your riding.

You must not carry a pillion passenger or pull a trailer unless you have a full motorcycle licence. However, all riders are allowed to carry loads and there are various methods available, including

- Panniers
- Top box
- Tank bag
- Luggage rack

In addition, a side-car outfit can be fitted to suitable machines. This provides additional carrying capacity for passengers and loads. This part covers the problems and techniques of carrying passengers and loads.

The topics covered

- Carrying a passenger
- Carrying a load
- Side-car outfits
- Towing a trailer

Carrying a passenger

Legal requirements

Before you can carry a passenger you must comply with the law.

You're allowed to carry a pillion passenger only if

- You've passed your practical motorcycle test
- You hold a full motorcycle licence for the category of machine you're riding

To carry a passenger your motorcycle should have

- Rear footrests
- A proper passenger seat

Motorcycle adjustments

To cope with the extra load of a pillion passenger you should

- Inflate the tyres according to the maker's instructions
- Adjust the pre-load on the rear shock absorbers to allow for the extra weight
- Adjust the headlamp aim, if necessary

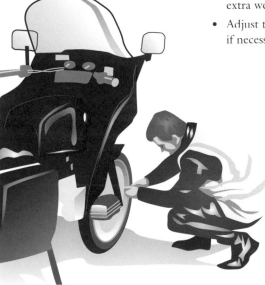

Passengers

If your passenger has never ridden pillion before, or you doubt their experience, instruct them to

- Sit astride the machine facing forwards
- Wear an approved motorcycle helmet, properly fastened
- Keep both feet on the passenger footrests until dismounting
- Keep a light but firm hold on your waist or the passenger grab handle (if fitted)
- Lean with you while going around bends or corners

Instruct your passenger not to

- Look behind or signal for you
- Lean to the side to see ahead. This might affect your balance and stability

Passenger's clothing   Your passenger's clothing should be

- Weatherproof and protective
- Bright and, if riding at night, reflective

Don't allow your passenger to wear a scarf or belt loosely fastened. These can get tangled in the wheel or drive chain and cause serious injury.

Riding techniques

Until you get used to carrying a passenger, ride with extra care. The passenger will affect

- Your balance, especially at low speeds
- Your ability to stop. The extra weight may increase your stopping distance. Allow a bigger gap when following another vehicle
- Your acceleration. You'll be slower getting moving so allow more room when emerging at junctions

Don't

- Carry young children on a motorcycle
- Ask your passenger to look behind or signal for you
- Accept any road or traffic information from your passenger without verifying it

Carrying a load

To carry a load on a motorcycle you can use

- Panniers
- Top box
- Tank bag
- Luggage rack

Panniers

There are two types of panniers available

- Rigidly fixed
- Throw-over saddlebag

Whichever type you use always make sure that the weight is evenly distributed. Uneven loading can lead to loss of stability.

Top box

A top box is fastened onto a rack behind the seat. It's easy and quick to use but has its limitations. The weight is carried high up and at the very back of the machine. Don't carry heavy loads in a top box because this can

- Reduce stability
- Cause low-speed wobble
- Cause high-speed weave

Tank bag

A tank bag is fastened on top of the fuel tank (or dummy tank) and can carry large loads. Take care that the tank bag doesn't interfere with your ability to steer.

Luggage rack

Make sure that any items strapped onto the luggage rack are securely fastened. A loose load could become tangled in the rear wheel and cause an accident.

Adjusting your motorcycle

Make any necessary adjustments to the

- Suspension
- Tyres
- Lights

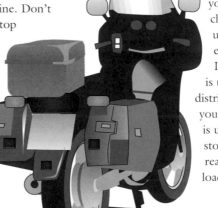

When riding with a load give yourself the chance to get used to the extra weight. If the load is unevenly distributed and your machine is unbalanced stop and rearrange the load.

Side-car outfits

If you want to fit a side-car

- Ask your dealer if your machine is suitable
- Make sure that, after fitting, the side-car is fixed correctly to the mounting points
- In the UK, side-cars should be fitted only on the left side of the machine if the machine is registered on or after 1 August 1981

Aligning the side-car

Make sure that the bike and side-car are correctly aligned. If they aren't the outfit will be difficult to control and probably dangerous.

Riding techniques

You must adapt your riding technique when riding a bike with a side-car. Keep your speed down until you've become used to the outfit.

On bends and when turning, the side-car outfit must be steered because you can't lean the machine over. This requires a deliberate push or pull on the handlebar.

On left-hand bends the side-car wheel will tend to lift as the weight is thrown outwards. This calls for special care and control.

Braking

Unless a brake is fitted to the side-car wheel the outfit will tend to pull to the right under heavy braking.

The extra weight of the side-car may increase the overall stopping distance.

Side-car outfits need special care on bends

Towing a trailer

You can only tow a trailer behind your motorcycle if

- You have a full motorcycle licence
- Your machine has an engine capacity exceeding 125cc
- The trailer doesn't exceed 1 metre (just over 3 feet) in width
- The distance between the rear axle of the motorcycle and the rear of the trailer is less than 2.5 metres (about 8 feet)
- The motorcycle is clearly marked with its kerbside weight
- The trailer is clearly marked with its unladen weight
- The laden weight of the trailer doesn't exceed 150kg or two-thirds of the kerbside weight of the motorcycle, whichever is less

You can't tow

- More than one trailer
- A trailer if you also have a side-car fitted
- A trailer carrying a passenger

When you tow a trailer remember that

- You must obey the speed limit restrictions which apply for all vehicles towing trailers
- Your stopping distance may be increased
- Any load in the trailer must be secure
- The trailer must be fitted to the machine correctly

Don't forget it's there!

A motorcycle needs routine attention and maintenance to keep it in a roadworthy condition. Learning how to carry out routine maintenance yourself will save you time and money.

Many routine maintenance jobs are straightforward and explained in the owner's handbook. More difficult tasks may need to be referred to your dealer.

Rider training courses may include some mechanical instruction and advice on maintenance.

The topics covered

- Regular checks
- Brakes
- Wheels
- Tyres
- Engine
- Drive chain

Regular checks

You should check the following
items on a regular basis.

Controls

- Brakes
- Clutch
- Accelerator

Electrical systems

- Lights
- Horn
- Indicators

Suspension and steering

- Front forks
- Shock absorbers
- Head-stock bearings
- Tyres
- Wheels
- Drive chain (where fitted)

Fluid levels

- Engine oil
- Gearbox oil
- Brake fluid (hydraulic brakes)
- Battery electrolyte
- Engine coolant (liquid-cooled
  engines)

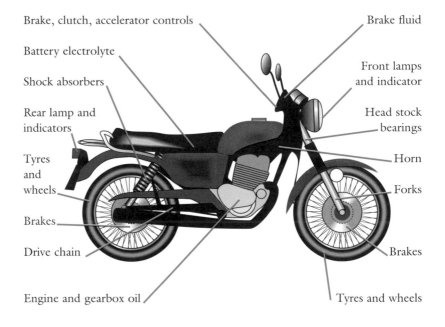

Brake, clutch, accelerator controls

Battery electrolyte

Shock absorbers

Rear lamp and indicators

Tyres and wheels

Brakes

Drive chain

Engine and gearbox oil

Brake fluid

Front lamps and indicator

Head stock bearings

Horn

Forks

Brakes

Tyres and wheels

Brakes

There are two types of braking system fitted to motorcycles

- Mechanically operated
- Hydraulically operated

With use, various parts of the braking system will wear and need adjustment or replacement.

Mechanically operated

If your motorcycle has mechanically operated brake systems

- The strain on brake cables causes them to stretch, so periodic adjustment is necessary
- Keep the pivots and cables lubricated to maintain efficiency

Hydraulically operated

If your motorcycle has hydraulic brakes, check

- Brake fluid levels regularly
- Couplings and joints for leaks

Brake pads and shoes gradually wear during use. Check and replace them as necessary.

Wheels

Motorcycles are fitted with either

- Spoked wheels
- Alloy wheels
- Pressed steel wheels (small-wheeled machines only)

Check that the wheels are running 'true'. Spin each wheel in turn and watch where it passes a suspension arm or mudguard stay. If the wheel is buckled this will show up.

Check spoked wheels for loose or broken spokes, and alloy wheels for cracks or visible damage.

Regularly check wheel nuts and bolts for tightness.

Have your wheels balanced regularly by an authorised dealer or tyre fitter.

Tyres

Pressure and condition

Incorrectly inflated tyres can cause

- Loss of stability
- Reduced grip
- Increased tyre wear

Check your tyres' pressures

- At least weekly
- When the tyres are cold

The correct tyre pressure settings can be found in the owner's manual.

You might have to increase the tyres' pressures

- When carrying a pillion passenger
- When carrying loads
- When riding at sustained high speeds

In addition, check your tyres for

- Tread depth and uneven tread wear
- Cuts or splits
- Small stones, glass or any other object stuck in the tyre
- Grease or oil which could affect the tyres' grip

If there's any sign that the tyres have been damaged they should be replaced.

Regulations

You must not use any tyre that has

- A cut longer than 25 mm or 10% of the width of the tyre, whichever is the greater
- A cut which is deep enough to reach the ply
- A lump, bulge or tear caused by the part failure of its structure
- Any exposed ply or cord
- Been recut

Minimum tread

The base of any groove which showed in the original tread must be seen clearly.

The grooves on the tread pattern of all tyres must not be less than 1 mm deep, forming a continuous band at least three-quarters of the breadth of the tread and all the way around.

The entire original tread must be visible, with a continuous band all of the way around.

Motorcycles less than 50cc

If your motorcycle has an engine capacity of less than 50cc the tread of the tyre may be less than 1 mm *if* the base of any groove which showed in the original tread can be seen clearly.

Punctures

If your machine suddenly becomes unstable a puncture might be the cause. If this happens or a tyre bursts

- Don't brake suddenly
- Hold the handlebars firmly
- Close the throttle to make the machine slow down
- Try to keep a straight course
- Stop gradually at the side of the road

A punctured tyre should be properly repaired or replaced.

When replacing a tyre

- Fit a tyre that is recommended by the manufacturer
- Buy the correct type. Some machines require a different type of tyre on the front and back wheel
- Change the inner tube at the same time (if you have tubed tyres)
- Make sure that the front and back tyre are compatible
- Check the rim for sharp objects
- Ensure that any liner fitted on a spoked wheel is in good condition

Wrongly matched tyres or incorrect tyre pressure can cause

- Loss of stability
- Wobble and/or weave

New tyres have a shiny finish which can reduce their grip. Ride carefully until this shinyness wears off, especially on wet or slippery roads. This could take up to 100 miles.

Engine

A properly maintained engine will

- Start more easily
- Use less fuel
- Be more reliable
- Give optimum performance
- Have lower exhaust emissions

Items which will affect the engine performance include

- Spark plugs
- Ignition settings
- Air filter
- Carburettor setings
- Valve clearances

If you aren't confident in your ability to maintain your engine entrust the work to your dealer.

Exhaust

Exhaust systems

- Must not be excessively noisy or altered
- Must be securely fitted

On motorcycles first used after 1 January 1985 the silencer must be marked and of an approved type.

Drive chain

The rear wheel on motorcycles is driven by either

- A chain or belt
- A 'prop' shaft

Drive chains wear and require frequent adjustment and lubrication. Use a special motorcycle chain lubricant which is made for this purpose.

If the chain is worn or slack it can jump off the sprocket and lock the rear wheel.

The drive chain needs to be adjusted until the free play is as specified in the handbook.

When you've adjusted the chain tension you need to check the rear wheel alignment. Marks by the chain adjusters may be provided to make this easy.

The theory test will gauge your knowledge and understanding of riding theory. A sound knowledge of the theory is essential to a better understanding of practical riding skills.

To help you to learn the theory a wide range of products is available including books, videos and CD-ROMs.

This part explains how to apply and take the theory test.

The topics covered

- **Your questions answered**
- **The pass certificate**

Your questions answered

Who's affected?

All provisional driving licence-holders will have to pass the theory test before a booking for a practical test will be accepted.

If you hold a full car licence but are riding on the provisional motorcycle entitlement this provides you don't have to take the theory test.

Ready for your test?

Make sure that you're well prepared before you attempt the test. Good preparation will save you time and money.

Theory test sessions are available during weekdays, evenings and on Saturdays. A test appointment will normally be available for you within about two weeks.

There are theory test centres throughout Great Britain and Northern Ireland. You can find out where your local centre is from

- A driver training organisation
- A DSA driving test centre
- The telephone information line 0645 000 555

If you have special needs please state this on your application form. Every effort will be made to ensure that the appropriate arrangements are made for you.

If you pass

You'll be notified of the result of your test within two weeks. If you've passed you'll be issued with a pass certificate.

If you fail

If you haven't passed the theory test then you must retake it.

The pass certificate

The pass certificate will be valid for two years. You must take and pass the practical test within that time or you'll have to take the theory test again.

Note:
Between 1 July 1996 and 1 January 1997 a special arrangement to allow candidates to take the practical test first, if necessary, is in place. To gain a full licence the theory test must be passed within six months.

The regulations which govern motorcycle riding call for

- Compulsory Basic Training (CBT) to be taken before you ride unaccompanied on the road

- The theory test to be passed before you apply for the practical motorcycle test (after 1 January 1997)

The main requirements of the motorcycle test are the same as for the driving test. You can find the officially recommended syllabus for learning to ride in the book *The Driving Test* (HMSO), available in most good bookshops.

The topics covered

- **Your questions answered**
- **Applying**
- **Attending**
- **Your test motorcycle**
- **The eyesight test**
- **Making progress**
- **Controlling your speed**
- **Awareness and anticipation**
- **Special exercises**
- **Disqualified riders**
- **The extended test**

Your questions answered

What's the purpose of the test?

The practical test is designed to gauge whether you can ride safely. The test ensures that all riders reach a minimum standard.

What's the order of the test?

The eyesight test is first. If your eyesight isn't up to the standard the test won't continue.

After the eyesight test the order is up to the examiner.

How long will the test last?

About 35 minutes.

What will the test include?

Apart from general riding, your test will include

- An eyesight test
- Special exercises, such as an emergency stop

What about the special exercises?

The first special exercise is usually the emergency stop. This normally comes after a short ride.

The examiner will be as helpful as possible and will

- Ask you to pull up on the left
- Explain any one of the special exercises and ask you to carry it out

Make sure that you understand. If you aren't sure about anything, ask! The examiner will explain again.

You'll be required to demonstrate the other set exercises while riding over the test route.

How the examiner will test you

Before the test you'll be fitted with

- A radio receiver on a belt
- An earpiece designed to be worn under your helmet

When you're taking the test the examiner will follow you either on a motorcycle or in a car (except during the emergency stop exercise). At the end of the test your examiner will ask you a question about carrying a pillion passenger on your machine.

What the examiner will expect

The examiner will want to see that you ride safely and competently under various road and traffic conditions.

You'll be

- Given directions clearly and in good time
- Asked to carry out set exercises

The examiner will be understanding and sympathetic and will make every effort to put you at ease.

How should you ride during the test?

The examiner will be looking for an overall safe ride. If you make a mistake, don't worry. It might not affect the result.

Does the standard of the test vary?

NO! All examiners are trained to carry out tests to the same standard.

Test routes

- Are as uniform as possible
- Include a range of typical road and traffic conditions

Are examiners supervised?

Examiners are frequently supervised by a senior officer. If a senior officer is present at your test, don't worry.

The senior officer

- Checks that the examiner is testing you properly
- Won't interfere with the test or the result

Passing the test

You'll pass if you can satisfy the examiner that you can

- Ride safely
- Comply with correct road procedure
- Obey traffic signs
- Carry out the set exercises correctly

When you've passed

You'll be allowed to ride

- Without L plates
- Unsupervised
- On motorways

The size of motorcycle you'll be licensed to ride immediately after passing your test will depend on the machine you've used to take the test. See Part Two.

Applying

To apply for your practical motorcycle test fill out an application form, DL26, which is available from any

- DSA Area Office
- Driving test centre

Full details of all fees can be obtained from DSA Area Offices or any driving test centre.

Send your application to the DSA at Newcastle. Complete the form and send it with the appropriate fee to the PO Box and postcode **for your Area** (see the list at the back of this book). Your application may be delayed if you address it incorrectly.

Alternatively, you can book your test appointment over the telephone using most major credit and debit cards. You'll find the telephone numbers at the back of this book.

If you wish to take your test in Wales using the Welsh language, please indicate this on the form.

Apply well before you want to be tested and give the earliest date when you think you'll be ready.

Send your CBT certificate with your application. If you don't, you must show it to the examiner when you attend your test. If you fail to do so your test may not be conducted.

Special circumstances

To make sure that enough time is allowed for your test it would help the DSA to know if you

- Are profoundly deaf
- Are restricted in any way in your movements
- Have any disability which may affect your riding

If any of these apply to you, please write this on your application form.

If you can't speak English or are deaf you may bring an interpreter. If you intend doing this, please tell us on the application form.

Your test appointment

Your DSA Area Office will send you an appointment card. This will give you

- The time and date of the appointment
- The address of the driving test centre
- Other important information

You should normally receive notification within two weeks of your application. If you don't, contact the DSA Area Office without delay.

Postponing your test appointment

Contact the DSA Area Office where you booked your test if

- The date or time on the card isn't suitable
- You want to postpone or cancel the test

You must give at least ten clear working days' notice (that is, two weeks – longer if there's a bank holiday) not counting

- The day the Area Office received your request
- The day of the test

If you don't give enough notice you'll lose your fee.

Saturday and evening tests

Tests are available at some driving test centres on Saturdays and weekday evenings. These test times have a higher fee.

Attending

Make sure that you have your driving licence with you and that you've signed it. You'll have to show it to your examiner and sign a declaration that your machine is insured. If you don't have your licence or it isn't signed your examiner may not be able to conduct the test.

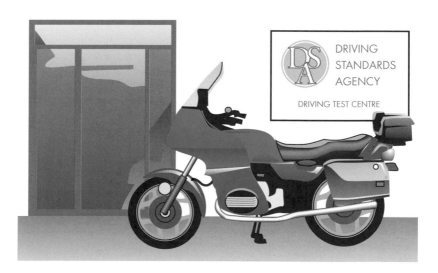

DRIVING STANDARDS AGENCY

DRIVING TEST CENTRE

Your test motorcycle

Make sure that the motorcycle you intend to ride during your test is

- Legally roadworthy and has a current test certificate, if it's over the prescribed age
- Fully covered by insurance for you to ride and for its present use
- Of the correct engine size/power output for the category of test that you're taking
- Properly licensed with the correct tax disc displayed
- Displaying L plates (or D plates in Wales) which are visible from the front and rear

If you overlook any of these your test may be cancelled and you could lose your fee.

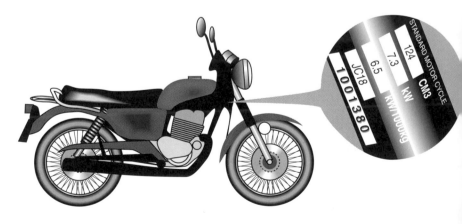

The eyesight test

What the test requires

You must satisfy the examiner that in good daylight you can read a vehicle number plate

- with letters 79.4 mm (3.1 in) high
- At a distance of 20.5 metres (about 67 feet)

If you need glasses or contact lenses to read the number plate you must wear them during the test and whenever you ride.

How the examiner will test you

Before you mount your motorcycle the examiner will ask you to read the number plate of a vehicle at a little over the prescribed distance.

If you're unable to read the number plate the examiner will measure the exact distance and repeat the test.

If you fail the eyesight test

If you can't read the number plate at the measured distance

- Your eyesight isn't up to the standard necessary to ride on the road
- Your test won't continue

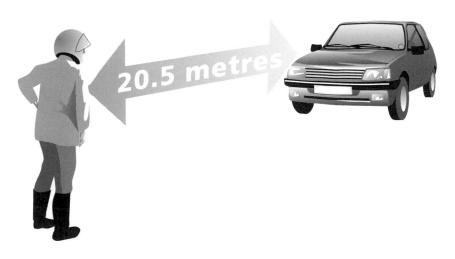

20.5 metres

Making progress

What the test requires

You must

- Be able to move off safely and under control
- Make progress along the road
- Ride at a speed appropriate to the road and traffic conditions
- Move off at junctions as soon as it's safe to do so

How the examiner will test you

For this aspect of riding there's no set exercise. The examiner will watch your riding and will want to see you

- Making appropriate progress along the road
- Keeping up with the traffic
- Showing confidence and sound judgement

Skills you need

You must be able to choose the correct speed for

- The type of road
- The type and density of the traffic
- The weather and visibility

Approach all hazards at a safe speed without

- Being too cautious
- Interfering with the progress of other traffic

Faults you must avoid

You must not

- Ride too slowly – you could hold up traffic
- Be over-cautious and stop or wait when it's safe and normal to proceed

Controlling your speed

What the test requires

You must make good, safe progress along the road bearing in mind

- Road conditions
- Traffic
- Weather
- Road signs and speed limits

How the examiner will test you

For this aspect of riding there's no special exercise. The examiner will watch carefully how you control your speed as you ride.

Skills you need

You must

- Take great care in the use of speed
- Make sure that you can stop safely well within the distance that you can see to be clear
- Leave a safe distance between yourself and other vehicles
- Leave extra distance on wet or slippery roads
- Ride within the speed limits

Faults you must avoid

- Riding too fast for the road or traffic conditions
- Changing your speed erratically

Awareness and anticipation

You must be aware of other road users at all times. You should always think and plan ahead so that you can

- Judge what other road users are going to do
- Predict how their actions will affect you
- React in good time

What the test requires

You must show

- Awareness of and consideration for all road users
- Anticipation of possible danger and concern for safety

For example, the following groups of vulnerable road users should be considered.

Pedestrians

- Give way to pedestrians when turning from one road to another
- Take particular care with the very young, the disabled and the elderly. They may not have seen you and could step out suddenly

Cyclists

- When crossing bus or cycle lanes, take special care

- Children on bicycles can be unaware of the danger of traffic. Give them plenty of room and try to anticipate any danger

Animals

- Show care and consideration for people in charge of animals, especially horse riders

Faults you must avoid

- Always reacting to road and traffic conditions at the last moment rather than anticipating them
- Showing irritation with other road users
- Sounding your horn aggressively
- Revving your engine or edging forward when waiting for pedestrians to cross

Special exercises

Emergency stop

You need to

- Apply the front brake just before the rear
- Apply both brakes effectively
- Stop the machine as quickly as possible without locking either wheel

Walking with your machine

Your examiner will ask you to put your machine on its stand. You'll then be asked to take your machine off its stand and to walk with it, without the aid of the engine.

U-turn

At some stage the examiner will ask you to perform a U-turn and stop on the other side of the road. Rear observation into the blind area is vital just before you carry out the manoeuvre.

Angle start

At some stage the examiner will ask you to pull up just before a parked vehicle. Before you move off again, make sure that you check

- To the rear and into the blind area
- Ahead to see there's no danger from approaching traffic

If an angle start occurs normally during the test you may not be asked to do it again.

Slow riding

You'll be asked to ride along at a walking speed for a short distance. This exercise tests your control, balance and observation. If you've already ridden slowly, such as in traffic, you may not be asked to carry out this exercise.

Hill start

The examiner might ask you to pull up on an uphill gradient. When moving off, your machine could be slower accelerating. You'll need to remember this when judging the moment to ride off.

Disqualified riders

Tough penalties exist for anyone convicted of dangerous riding or driving.

Courts will impose an extended test on anyone convicted of dangerous driving offences. They can also impose an extended test on anyone convicted of other offences involving obligatory disqualification.

If you've been disqualified for other endorsable offences the courts can order a normal-length test before you can recover a full licence.

Recovering a full licence

A rider subject to a retest can apply for a provisional licence at the end of the disqualification period. The normal rules for provisional licence-holders will apply.

A rider doesn't have to undertake CBT if

- They already hold a CBT completion certificate

- Before disqualification they had passed the full motorcycle or moped test

The theory test must be passed before applying for either an extended or a normal-length test.

The extended test

The extended motorcycle or moped test involves over 60 minutes' riding time. The test routes cover a wide variety of roads, usually including dual carriageways.

A rider has to

- Maintain a satisfactory standard throughout the extended test period

- Cope with a wide range of road and traffic conditions

The examiner will apply the same standard of assessment as for an ordinary test. However, the extra time and wide variety of road and traffic conditions make the extended test more demanding. Candidates should make sure that they're well prepared before applying.

Higher fees

The higher fee for the extended motorcycle test reflects the extra length of the test.

DSA THE MOTORCYCLING MANUAL

DSA Head Office

Stanley House
Talbot Street
Nottingham
NG1 5GU
Tel: 0115 955 7600

DSA mail is initially processed at Newcastle. Driving tests are then booked at DSA's five Area Offices. The addresses and telephone numbers of the Area Offices are

London and South-East

Postal applications to:
DSA, PO Box 289
Newcastle-upon-Tyne
NE99 1WE

Telephone bookings by credit or debit card and other enquiries
Tel: 0171 957 0957
Fax: 0171 468 4550
Recorded message:
0171 468 4530

Midland and Eastern

Postal applications to:
DSA, PO Box 287
Newcastle-upon-Tyne
NE99 1WB

Telephone bookings by credit or debit card and other enquiries
Tel: 0121 697 6700
Fax: 0121 697 6750
Recorded message:
0121 697 6730

Wales and Western

Postal applications to:
DSA, PO Box 286
Newcastle-upon-Tyne
NE99 1WA

Telephone bookings by credit or debit card and other enquiries
Tel: 0122 258 1000
Fax: 0122 258 1050
Recorded message:
0122 258 1030

Northern

Postal applications to:
DSA, PO Box 280
Newcastle-upon-Tyne
NE99 1FP

Telephone bookings by credit or debit card and other enquiries
Tel: 0191 201 4000
Fax: 0191 201 4010
Recorded message:
0191 201 4100

Scotland

Postal applications to:
DSA, PO Box 288
Newcastle-upon-Tyne
NE99 1WD

Telephone bookings by credit or debit card and other enquiries
Tel: 0131 529 8580
Fax: 0131 529 8589
Recorded message:
0131 529 8592